CHESS IS
CHILD'S PLAY

by Laura Sherman and Bill Kilpatrick

CHESS IS
CHILD'S PLAY
Teaching Techniques That Work

by **Laura Sherman**
and **Bill Kilpatrick**

MONGOOSE
Press

Publisher: Mongoose Press
1005 Boylston Street, Suite 324
Newton Highlands, MA 02461
info@mongoosepress.com
www.MongoosePress.com

ISBN: 978-1936277315
Library of Congress Control Number: 2012930145

Distributed to the trade by National Book Network
custserv@nbnbooks.com, 800-462-6420
For all other sales inquiries please contact the publisher.

Editing: Dr. Alexey W. Root
Proofreading: Jorge Amador
Photography: Kristy Mann
Layout & Pre-Press: Al Dianov

First edition
Printed in the United States of America

*

To our children
And our children's children.
May you gain as much from the game of chess as we have!

*

We would like to thank all the children who trained with us throughout the years. Their hard work and eagerness inspired us to write this book to help their brothers, sisters, friends and classmates (as well as many parents) learn to play the game of chess.

In addition we are grateful to Dr Alexey W. Root, Jorge Amador and Mongoose Press for their suggestions that enhanced our book.

We would like to thank the Internet Chess Club (www.chessclub.com) for allowing us to use their diagram design in our book.

And finally, Kristy Mann, who contributed her photographic skills and aesthetic brilliance sparked by her own lifelong appreciation for chess. Chess and art will always share the same stage.

CONTENTS

This isn't a children's book. That's why there aren't any colorful illustrations or cartoon characters.

It is a book written for parents. It's written for you!

For those parents who don't know how to play chess, this book will teach you and your child together, in a way that is easy and fun for both of you.

Some experienced chess-playing parents would love to share this game with their young children, but don't know how to introduce them to chess.

This book is designed to help chess masters and novices alike. So, if you are an excellent chess player, this book is for you, too!

We have included little anecdotes throughout called "Coffee Talk." These stories came from our teaching experiences through the years.

We also have tips labeled "Coach's Corner," which are extra stories or techniques based on our experiences.

At the end of each chapter, we have a troubleshooting section, anticipating problems you may encounter. We offer solutions that have worked with our children and students.

We hope that you enjoy this book and have many fun lessons with your children!

Laura and Bill

Laura's Bio

Laura Sherman is a freelance writer and chess coach. Together with her husband, Dan, she founded Your Chess Coach in Florida. Laura and Dan have taught hundreds of children the wonders of chess.

Laura and Dan met through tournament chess in Los Angeles, California. At the time, they both had the same national rating, which Laura found to be terribly romantic.

Today they have three young children. When their first child turned four, Laura started teaching him chess. When she successfully taught him to play, she began teaching his classmates, perfecting the techniques to work on any child.

Laura also began exploring teaching techniques for her two-year-old daughter, who expressed a strong interest after watching her brother play many games. Laura then taught her daughter's preschool schoolmates, giving them an introduction to the game. The next logical step was to write a book that would teach parents to teach their young children!

Bill's Bio

Bill Kilpatrick became a serial entrepreneur by creating many successful business ventures.

He developed advanced chess skills at any early age playing game after game with his mother, father, and sisters. In high school, Bill helped coach his own team, and as a crew of underdogs they swiftly rose to become a dominant force, winning the Florida State and Southeastern U.S. Championships.

He took the knowledge that was given to him as a young man, and shared it with others by building businesses with the common theme of teaching or coaching diverse skills. The ventures include acting, business management, software development, creative writing, and – of course – chess.

Why Chess?

1

hess is far more than just a fun game for bright kids.

Numerous studies have been done around the world, exploring the relationship between chess and education. The results are astounding.

Some governments have made chess a mandatory part of children's education. Many homeschoolers embrace chess as a teaching tool.

Why is chess so highly valued?

The fact is, chess makes kids smarter!

In this chapter, we will summarize some of the findings from our research on the benefits of chess in education, and include a few of our own observations as well.

Coach's Corner

The Venezuelan experiment, "Learning to Think Project," tested whether chess could help increase a child's intelligence. The study ran four years, testing over 4,000 second graders.

The IQ of both the boys and the girls from this study improved after studying chess!

Chess gives children problem-solving skills

Throughout life, one of the most valuable skills a person can have is the ability to solve problems. Parents want their children to be able to find and select the best solutions for every given situation they will encounter out in the real world.

A weaker mind waits for others to solve problems for them. Such individuals lack the courage and skill to implement their own ideas. They become dependent upon others to solve their problems.

As a chess player, you face your opponent one-on-one. No one is allowed to whisper answers into your ear, or feed you game-winning moves.

Your child will start recognizing patterns. Children who have this ability are less likely to make the same mistake twice. They tend to learn more from their errors.

Chess helps children plan for unwanted surprises

We've all been caught off-guard in life at one time or another. When you're able to think quickly and have a few backup plans ready to go, life's unexpected surprises are never really a problem, just an inconvenience.

Every player has been surprised by a move their opponent made. It happens. The trick is to be able to handle the situation without crumbling, keeping a cool head.

When children study chess, they also learn to look at the world around them as it changes. They tailor their plans to the new situations that arise. As a result, they can take control of many more situations, often coming out the winner.

Chess gives children the ability to think ahead

Successful chess players think ahead, predicting and guiding the pieces' actions with the moves they make. They learn to envision future events.

Chess allows children to try out strategies for victory, learning what works and what doesn't.

Each chess move has consequences, plusses and minuses to consider. As your children gain experience, the effects their moves will create on the board pop to view more quickly for them. This ability guides your child to make the best decisions.

Every game of chess is a unique battle. You learn a lot from the experience, taking that knowledge to the next game. Your child will learn to do that in other areas of life, creating strategies to ensure continued success in their pursuits.

Chess gives children self-confidence

No one likes a braggart, but it's vital for our children to have a healthy self-confidence in life. They should always know they can accomplish whatever it is that they want to do.

In a world where children are often ignored and devalued, chess gives them a tremendous edge. Over the board, each player has a truly equal opportunity to come out ahead. There is no bias for age or physical size. You win because you outplay your opponent.

No one can ever take a win away from you.

When your child starts winning against adults, there is nothing that can take that self-confidence away from them. They have outplayed a grown-up!

They know that they can win at life too.

Chess teaches children to think outside the box

Some schools spend most of the time teaching children to think inside the box.

Rules of thumb are important. They give you guidelines. However, when you know what you're doing in a given area, you find you sometimes wind up ahead if you bend a rule or two. Sometimes you set a new standard, which others will follow.

Chess players learn to think outside the box!

If we're going to solve some of the enormous problems this world has, our children must be able to think outside the box. They will need to come up with many innovative solutions.

Chess teaches children how to win and lose graciously

It's important for our children not to "adapt" to failure or start accepting setbacks. That approach reduces a child's drive and determination.

However, when you win a game or lose a game in chess, it is proper etiquette to shake your opponent's hand and say, "Good game!" It is rare that you see players do anything else.

Children learn this quickly, as they become accustomed to winning and losing. If your child has trouble with losing, chess helps them get over that. After they play many, many games, they quickly see that they can't win them all.

We teach our students not to do a victory dance every time they win. They laugh a lot when we give this talk, but in the end they get it and even promote this idea to each other on the rare occasion that a student forgets.

How your child handles wins and losses in life as they grow up, makes an enormous difference. People always appreciate good sportsmanship.

Coffee Talk

Chess manners are important

A mother of a five-year-old boy called to say that her son had been home sick from school. To pass the time, he had asked to play chess with her. She agreed, and won.

She was astonished when her son reached out his hand and said, "Good one, mom!" Prior to learning chess, he would get very upset when he lost any game.

Chess gives children the ability to create their own possibilities

The chessboard is simply a grid with 64 squares. At the start of the game, it is filled with 32 pieces. When a child sits across from an opponent, the board and set becomes a playing field, filled with promise and adventure.

Children's imagination is enhanced through chess. They learn to create positions, put ideas into action, and see immediate results.

Through chess, your child will learn that it is possible to conquer many obstacles and challenges. Just knowing that they are able to flex creative muscles will open new doors for them as they tackle their life goals.

Chess gives children the ability to concentrate for extended periods

Some parents fear that their children can never master chess, because they can't sit still for very long. Fortunately, chess draws them into a special world, one that helps them focus their attention for long periods of time.

The ability to concentrate will help your child with their other studies. Once they become captivated by chess, their interests will soar in other subjects as well. As they focus their mind on various tasks, they will improve and "win" in those areas too.

Coffee Talk

Chess improves concentration

One child had a lot of trouble sitting still. He couldn't stay in his seat for more than a minute or two. After a few months, he played in one of our tournaments and was completely absorbed in his games for over an hour.

It wasn't an overnight transformation, but the improvement in his ability to concentrate was astounding!

Chess builds a sense of teamwork within children

The pieces on the board work together. If you keep moving just one piece, forgetting the others, you won't do well. Players learn to use the pieces together, creating a harmony of movement, controlling the game.

New players will often begin with their most powerful chess piece, thinking that piece can do the job of winning the game on its own. Beginners quickly learn that a piece cannot survive very long on its own in the battlefield.

Later in life, when your child joins the work force, they will either join teams or form teams to get work done. These teams will need to be organized and supported. Your child will need to learn their role within the organization, so that they can do the job well and advance.

When children learn to use all their pieces together on a chessboard, they will be building teams to create attacks and defend positions. They will learn to accomplish their goals with teamwork.

Chess inspires children to tackle difficult tasks

There will be times when your child sits down to play an opponent and the odds are against them, at least in their mind. Perhaps the other player is much older, even a grown-up. Maybe they will play an experienced tournament player, whose rating is much higher than theirs.

When they start winning these games, the ones they deemed "impossible" to win, they might start to realize that nothing is truly impossible.

If the children of our society consider that there is nothing they cannot do, we'll wind up with a next generation of problem solvers who can handle some of the issues that previous generations have left behind.

Coach's Corner

"The most wonderful thing about chess is the way it transforms people from the inside out," said New York educator John Kennedy.

"Once they're exposed to the instruction, kids get chess fever. And once they get hooked, their desire to apply themselves soars."

—" The Palm Report, "Christine Palm, 1990

What You Should Expect
FROM THE LESSONS

2

arents routinely report that chess is a wonderful bonding experience for parent and child. Your child will most likely remember these lessons for the rest of their lives.

Don't expect this book to teach everything about the game. Instead, we wish to help you get your young child started on their personal chess adventure. We'll help you give them a good foundation upon which they can build more knowledge. Knowledge also grows as they gain experience and study further.

Coach's Corner

There's usually a sweet fondness in a person's voice when they mention the parent or grandparent who taught them to play chess.

My father and I had many hours of fun over a chessboard.

— Laura

We'll give you an easy, step-by-step approach

We thoroughly embrace using a step-by-step approach when teaching children anything, and chess is no exception. If you sit down and tell your child how all the pieces move in ten minutes, you're likely to overwhelm them and they "won't like chess."

The remedy is to move things along at the right pace. Start with one piece and really teach your child all about it before moving on to the next.

There will be exercises for children of all ages

We're writing for the parents of younger children and older children alike. We've included special exercises for two-, three-, and four-year-olds as well.

The lessons for a two-year-old will be a bit different than for a ten-year-old. Some two-year-olds will be able to finish all the exercises given, while others might need to wait a year or two.

Older children usually progress faster than younger ones, but that isn't always the case. You need to move at the speed of your child. You'll know when they're ready to move on, if you're watching for the signs.

There aren't any hard-and-fast rules of what you can expect for any given age. We can tell you what we've seen with many children and students, but that doesn't mean your child will follow these guidelines:

- Age 1: Touching pieces and board. Picking up pieces and putting them into a bag. Putting them onto the board anywhere.
- Ages 2 and 3: Naming pieces and learning how some of the pieces move.
- Age 4: Fully able to do all the exercises in this book. Able to play a game with occasional errors in piece movement.
- Ages 5-7: Able to play a game without making many errors in piece move ment. Able to spot when a position is checkmate.
- Ages 8 and up: Rarely makes errors in piece movement. Can find checkmate in a game.

There will be tons of mini-games

This book is chock full of mini-games. They are very popular with children and will handle the plea, "But, I just want to play a game now!" Mini-games allow the child to play chess immediately, without thrusting them into a complete game situation that is overwhelming.

Children will readily play a mini-game, but they might resist doing an "exercise."

It is important to play each mini-game until you see that your child has accomplished the goal set out by the exercise. Don't skip them because you think they are too basic for your child. There are subtle nuances to be gained from each one that will form valuable building blocks of knowledge.

We'll help you troubleshoot problems

We have a pretty good idea of the problems that you might run into while teaching your child to play chess for the first time. We have taught hundreds of students, ranging from two years old on up, including a few dozen adults.

Chances are, if you run into trouble, we've seen it before and can help guide you through the lesson. You'll find a troubleshooting section at the end of most chapters.

Your child will learn to play chess

Chess has an unnecessary reputation for being a difficult game, a game only for geniuses. This isn't true. Anyone can play and anyone can become better at the game.

The key is to learn each step in the proper sequence. A child will embrace chess, asking for more lessons, as long as they enjoy the process and understand what you are teaching them.

Remember, there is no time clock here. It isn't a race.

You can re-interest a child in chess

If you have a child who started to learn chess and lost interest, you might be able to rekindle that interest by running through these exercises. Our approach will fill in missing gaps. Many beginners are missing the basic principles covered in this book.

Coach's Corner

I had a new student, an eight-year-old boy, who told me he was "very good" at chess. I paired him against another student and immediately noticed that he looked unhappy. I took him aside and quizzed him a bit, discovering he didn't really know how the pieces moved.

Once I knew this, it was an easy matter to catch him up to the rest of the class. Today he is enthusiastic about chess and doing very well.

— Laura

Tips on Teaching

3

lan to review this chapter often.

The first time you read these tips, they may appear to be a bit theoretical, especially if you're new to teaching chess.

Once you start teaching, though, they will be more helpful to you. These tips come from our experience and are designed to help your lessons run smoothly.

Coach's Corner

It's useful to sit back and look at your child while they play. You'll notice quite a lot about them. Their thoughts are impressive. I find most adults completely underestimate how intelligent and bright an "average" child really is.

— Bill

Stick to regular lessons, several times a week

If you really want your child to learn this game, you must commit to regular lessons two or three times a week. Sitting down once a week with your child will not work as well.

There is nothing wrong with nightly lessons. If your child wants to play each night, then by all means play!

Coach's Corner

I see students excel quickly in chess when they study outside our weekly classes.

If they only touch the set once a week, they usually don't do as well. They tend to make more errors.

— Laura

Consider the needs of their young body

Make sure your child has eaten well before the lesson. As with any study, your child cannot concentrate if their stomach is rumbling. No one can!

Another issue is sugar intake. If your child eats sugar right before the lesson, they will not be able to concentrate on the board for long. It is best to skip chess lessons the day after Halloween.

Also, if your child is overly tired the lesson will not go well. Teach children when they are fresh, not right before they are ready for bed or a nap.

The best plan is to combine chess lessons with some sort of exercise, especially when working with younger kids. Bring the set to the park or beach and teach them after they have run around for a while.

Coach's Corner

When I was first teaching my son, we would have a nice long swim in the ocean before we set up the board.

Doing a lesson first wouldn't have worked as well, because the temptation of the water would be vying for his attention.

— Laura

Keep the lessons short and fun

In order to keep chess lessons a positive experience, it is important to keep the lessons short and fun.

Your first lesson may only last five minutes. The important thing is to end before your child's attention veers off the chess lessons and on to something else.

As a general rule of thumb, the younger the child, the shorter the lessons.

Try not to make the mistake of going past that point where they'd rather go out and play and you're forcing them to learn.

Use real-life examples

Relating your lessons to the world around your children will help them understand what you are teaching. It may also bridge the gap to helping them apply some of the tidbits to their lives.

Coffee Talk

Chess in the real world

While looking out the window of the car one day, a boy exclaimed, "That car over there is moving like a bishop, and that one is moving like a rook!"

Another young student told his mother, "My friend's house is a bishop's move away from my school!"

Use very simple words

When you are teaching chess to your child, keep your language extra simple and to the point.

Avoid complex words that they might not know.

There are some chess words they will need to learn. Stick with these words during your lessons and encourage their use. These terms are important so that your child will be able to communicate more easily with other children or adults who play chess.

Keep your voice animated and real

If you think back to your favorite teachers or public speakers, they were probably very animated and sincere. Their conversations were realistic.

When you're working with children you can often be a bit over the top with your speech. Keep it real and true, but you can be a little zany and silly here and there if that's your style. Children often become more engaged in the subject when you are animated.

Children learn by watching

If you and your spouse are able to play chess with each other, your children can learn a lot by watching.

It will not only show them good moves and correct form, but it will spur them on to learn more. As they watch you, they will want to play more. You can also let them play with you, offering suggestions for moves.

Praise them often for a job well done

It is very important to let children know when they get answers correct, every time they do. Don't just assume that they know they got it right. They need to hear it. They love to know that you're proud of their accomplishments!

Coach's Corner

There are many ways to share excitement with a child when they do something right. For example, kids tend to light up and beam brightly with a "high-five."

Your unique style of loving acknowledgements becomes very personal and endearing for your child. It can do wonders to help them advance.

Turn your child into a chess coach

Allow your child to teach you or someone else whenever possible. Maybe they can teach a younger sibling or a grandparent. Teaching is a powerful way to learn.

Breaking down a subject, so that someone else can grasp it (something the best teachers always do), involves a challenging process that actually brings about a greater understanding for the teacher. Learning to teach a subject is an excellent way for your child to build their own understanding of the subject up to a high level.

You can develop your child's ability to teach and to subtly learn by turning around the actions of teaching.

For example, you can "test" their knowledge of the subject by having them instruct you, as if you were new to chess. Say, "Okay, now teach me (or show me) how to do that!"

Note: Some children will parrot the words, giving them back to you perfectly when you ask, but they have no clue what they just said. Watch out for this. You aren't looking for memorization of the chess moves and positions, only understanding.

Teaching children together

It is sometimes possible to teach two children together. This can succeed if they are at the same level of ability, and if they work well together. Even though they probably won't learn at the same rate, they will be able to play and practice with each other.

If one child is picking up concepts faster than the other (it may not be the older one who is doing so), you can handle this in one of two ways. One way would be to give them separate lessons, giving them each the chance to go at their own speed and have quality one-on-one time with you.

Another way is to allow the one progressing faster to help you teach the other. This will only work if the faster one is patient and willing to work at the other's speed. You'll have to observe them together to see if it is working. It's important that you're a part of the lessons.

If you choose this second option, make sure to give the faster child private lessons, moving forward at their speed, so they aren't held back or penalized for excelling.

Plan to repeat concepts for your child

Be prepared to repeat certain concepts over and over with your child. Don't get frustrated at this. It's all part of the process.

There are ways to do so which keep it fun and new. For instance, you can change the way you word things, finding new examples to give.

Each time you go over a rule or concept your child will digest more, picking up new aspects of the lesson.

Don't underestimate the number of times you might need to go over any one rule or idea.

Let them copy your movements

When you are working with a very young child, you may need to start by having them copy your movements. They will learn a lot from this process.

For instance, if you are teaching your child about a certain piece, you can simply make a move, put the piece back, and then ask them to make the exact same move. If they make a different move, simply show them the move again until they make the same exact move.

Start with the simplest move you can make with that piece. This is typically a short move, rather than a long move that puts the piece on the other side of the board.

Continue to move the piece to different squares, always putting it back where it came from. As long as they correctly copy you, make a new move, perhaps making it a little more difficult than the last.

If a move becomes too difficult for them, go back to an easier one. For instance, if you've moved a piece five squares away and they are having trouble copying you, go back to a move they were able to do (perhaps two or three squares away).

The thing to remember is that by copying your movements, they are making correct piece movements. It is a good step toward making the movements themselves.

Use the board and pieces, not the book

There is no need to show the diagrams in this book to your child. The main purpose of the diagrams is to show you what to teach your child. To teach them, use a real chessboard and pieces.

It's so much easier for children to learn with a three-dimensional board and set rather than from two-dimensional diagrams.

You should read this book first

If possible, read this book all the way through first and then start teaching your child. At a minimum, read through these tips and the entire chapter you're working on. It's best for you to be familiar with the game, as well as this style of teaching.

Do a rapid review of the last lesson before starting a new one

Even if you give your child nightly lessons, they will probably need a review of the last lesson before starting the next. This process can be very quick. If your child needs to work on a specific skill then spend some time covering it.

Go back to early steps if they're making lots of mistakes

If your child is having trouble with a section and can't seem to get the information, it is always a good idea to go to an earlier exercise and see if they could use more practice.

There is no race to get through the book. The important thing is that your child learns each lesson and enjoys the game of chess.

Anticipate your child's speed

Once your child has a certain concept down for one piece, they might quickly understand the similar concept when applied to another piece. For that reason, the lessons may go much faster for these pieces.

Watch for signs that your child understands the concepts given.

The speed of advancement in understanding piece movement is nowhere near as important as the thoroughness of their understanding of piece movement.

Moving ahead at a nice speed (for them) makes things fun for both of you.

Aim to have them always give the right answer

Ask questions that your child can correctly answer based on the information that they have. Whenever you pose a question to your child, you should expect them to get the right answer. Likewise, make sure any problem you give is one that they can solve correctly.

You're not asking questions to try to trip them up.. Ask questions that your child is highly likely to be able to answer.

Avoid asking your child questions that you aren't sure they know. It's better to start by showing them the correct answers, before asking them to demonstrate a concept they've never seen before.

This approach leads to a healthy self-confidence.

Instead of correcting your child, show them what they need to know

If your child makes an error, it is best to simply show them what they're missing, rather than tell them that they're wrong. Try to lead them to the right answer.

For instance, if your child makes an incorrect piece movement, show them three to five correct moves with the piece. Then ask them to show you how the piece moves again.

When you ask the question this time they'll feel good that they got the answer right.

Stick with a standard chess set

There are many chess sets available in stores. Most are completely wrong for a child.

Since your child is new to chess, you want the boards and pieces to make it easy to see what's going on.

Experienced chess players never use strange, non-standard sets. In fact, tournaments will not allow them.

Coach's Corner

I remember learning chess as a young child with a standard set. Years later when I played in tournaments, I noticed some of the other kids making unusual mistakes in some of their games. They were using strange pieces their parents had given them. I helped convince the other kids on my team to always use standard pieces.

— Bill

<u>The best pieces</u>

The best pieces are the standard design called "Staunton," named after a famous English chess master from the 1800's, Howard Staunton. These are the pieces in all the photographs within this book.

A weighted plastic set with a felt bottom works well for children who are young and just learning. The pieces are easy to grasp, feel good in the hand, and are very durable. In addition, they are inexpensive and the pieces are very easy to replace (sometimes they come with a guarantee).

As your child becomes more experienced, you can invest in a wooden set. These are a favorite at chess tournaments.

Chess sets are measured by the size of the king, which should stand about 3.75 inches tall for a 20-inch board. The rest of the pieces are proportional to the king.

The best boards

The best boards are simple in design, with colors that are pleasing (not jarring) to the eye.

One of the best options is a vinyl, roll-up board, forest green and white (which is a soft cream color), with 2.25-inch squares. They are inexpensive and very durable. You can even take them to the park or beach.

Where to get the best chess sets

Visit us at www.ChessIsChildsPlay.com for information on where to get the best chess sets.

What to avoid

If possible, do not purchase:

- Boards or pieces which use unusual colors
- Boards and pieces that are too big or too small
- Pieces that have a character theme
- Boards that are too ornate
- Pieces that are hollow or lightweight
- Pieces that are made from breakable material (like glass or stone)

For instance, you should avoid the old checkers sets, which come with a cardboard, red and black board. These do not make for good chessboards, because they are very hard on the eyes. Plus, it can be confusing to have the red squares represent the "light" squares. They aren't very light.

There are many playful themed sets available as well. While they can be fun, these are very confusing for a child just learning about the game. "Which one is the bishop again, mom?" isn't a question you want them to have to ask!

Coach's Corner

I've seen some amazing sets over the years. My father had a hand-carved wooden set, which depicted people as the pieces.

As a child I enjoyed looking at it, but I knew it was only meant for decoration. It sat on display for us to admire.

— Laura

The teeny-tiny sets available in stores are only meant for travel and should not be used for learning. When a set is really small, the pieces are hard to pick up and move around. Your child will knock over pieces as they reach to make a move. You'll probably do the same thing. It gets old fast.

As your child becomes more familiar with the game, they will find comfort in the familiarity of their pieces. It is a good idea to start out with ones that are the correct shape, weight, and material.

For experienced chess players

If you already know how to play chess, these techniques can make it much easier for you to teach your children.

You'll be able to make up exercises to complement the ones given here. It will be easy for you to set up realistic positions for the various steps along the way.

The primary thing you need to keep in mind is to hold back your desire to teach too much at once. It takes discipline and patience not to teach concepts that are too advanced for your child's level.

If you stick to the sequence given in this book, making sure they are really getting everything you're teaching along the way, you won't go wrong.

Special Exercises
FOR TWO-TO FOUR-YEAR-OLDS

4

hen you teach a child who is two, three, or four years of age, you usually need to spend more time on games designed to orient the child to the pieces and the board. If they get through these drills, move on to the first piece and see how they do.

If they're not ready, hold off until they are. You'll know they are ready for the next step because they will try to follow your directions to learn what you're teaching them.

Four-year-olds tend to move through these exercises much faster than two- or three-year-olds. But it all depends on the child. Some can run through all these drills in one or two lessons.

A two- or three-year-old might spend a few months on this chapter.

You should probably skip these steps for children aged five and up. Simply start with the chapter titled, "The Rook."

Naming the pieces

One of the first steps for your child is to learn the names of the pieces.

You will need to be very familiar with these names yourself, so that you can teach them to your child.

This step may take a while and may span several lessons.

If you're working with a very young child, plan to introduce only two pieces in the first lesson.

Step 1: This is a rook!
Start by keeping all the pieces in the bag (or box). If they are out on the table, they can be a distraction.

Pull out a rook and hand it to your child. Say, "This is a rook!" You want to make sure your child really looks at it and touches it.

Have your child repeat the word, "rook."

Hand them another rook and ask, "What is this?" If they need help, let them know it is a rook and have them repeat the word, "rook." Pull out another rook and another, asking your child what each piece is called. Your child will end up with all four rooks.

Coffee Talk

Shout it out!

Sometimes very young children will need encouragement to speak up. They aren't certain enough in their own voice for it to be audible.

One two-year-old girl was very shy. She whispered, "rook," very quietly when asked. However, when she was told she could shout it out, she did so, grinning happily about it. After that, she spoke at full volume.

Step 2: This is a bishop!
Next pull out a bishop and say, "This is a bishop!"

Have your child look at the piece. Ask them to compare it to the rook, telling you what makes it different from the rook.

Have them say the word, "bishop." Then hand your child the bishop.

Pull out another bishop and ask, "What's this?" Do this with all four bishops from the set. It doesn't matter if they are black or white bishops.

Step 3: Please pass me a piece
Now they have four rooks and four bishops near them. Point to the rook. Say, "Please pass me a rook." (Or you can say, "Please give me the rook," or "Now, hand me the rook.")

Usually by now, young children have forgotten the name of the first piece they worked with, so the reminder helps them.

When they hand you the rook, praise them for getting it right.

Now point to the bishop and say, "Please pass me a bishop" or one of the above variations of that request.

Then, without pointing, say, "Pass me another bishop."

Now ask for a rook. If they hand you a bishop, thank them and then point to the rook and say, "Is that a rook?" When you get their agreement that it is, say, "Please pass me a rook."

Go back and forth, asking for the pieces until you have all eight back again.

If you feel that they need more work with this (if they made some errors), start back again with, "What is this?" and hand them the piece. When they have all the pieces, ask for them back, one at a time.

This is often a good time to end the lesson for the day. Remember you always want to end when they are having fun and actively learning. If you make a mistake and go past this point, just end the lesson as soon as you can.

Step 4: Your child asks you for a piece
If you're starting a new lesson for the day, it is important to remind your child about the rook and the bishop. Have them point these two pieces out to you. If you feel they need more of a review, repeat the steps from the previous lesson.

If you feel that they have this down, tell them to ask you for a piece. They can choose which one they want, but they need to ask for it by name (rather than simply pointing to it). If they point to a piece, ask, "What is that piece called?"

When they have all the pieces, ask them to pass the pieces back to you one at a time, naming them each time.

When you can see that they are confident with the rook and bishop, move on to the next piece.

Step 5: This is a knight and a pawn!
Now introduce the knight to your child. This is often a child's favorite piece, because it looks like a horse. They may in fact want to call it a horse (or horsey), but it is good to get them used to calling it a knight.

If you consistently call it a knight, they will catch on. You don't need to correct them much or make a big deal about it. Just make sure you call it by the right name.

Play the same set of games with them, as in the exercises above, but include the knight. When they have it down, introduce the pawn in the same way. Again, have them touch the pawn and tell you what makes it different from the other pieces.

Once you have all four pieces in play, you can create little naming games based on the ones given above. It really doesn't matter how you do it, the idea is to get used to giving each piece its correct name.

When they can properly name these four pieces, end the lesson.

Step 6: This is a queen!
Now is a good time to introduce the queen. You can point out that it has a crown on its head. This can help them identify this piece.

Have them hold the queen and tell you that it is a queen.

Ask them what is different about the queen from the other pieces. There are many differences, but a key one is that it is taller than any of the others that you've named so far.

Now play the same kind of games you did in the previous step, but add in the queens.

Note: Some sets come with an extra queen for both sides. If this is the case, use all four queens from the set.

Step 7: This is a king!
Now show your child a king. Have them notice the difference between the king and the queen. It is a good idea to use a standard design, so that your child can learn to look for the king's cross. Other designs of pieces are tricky to tell apart.

If you look at them from the bottom, they pretty much look alike. It is the top that sets them apart.

Stand the two pieces on the table and ask your child, "Which piece is taller?" Make sure they notice that the king is a little taller.

Next take turns handing them a king and a queen, quizzing them on their names. When they can tell the difference, add in another piece. Keep adding pieces, until they are comfortable with all six pieces.

It is possible that you will need to end the lesson before you're done with this step. Remember you want to keep it fun and light. If they're cheerful and the lesson has lasted 20 minutes, it's a good idea to put the pieces away for the day.

Step 8: The Naming Game
In-between lessons it is a fun game to see how many pieces your child can name, without looking at the pieces. You can do this in the car or at the park. It's a little like trying to name the seven dwarfs.

The first few times they may only be able to get one or two names on their own. This is to be expected. Just help them come up with the rest (maybe giving hints to remind them).

It could take a few weeks until they have this down. When they can name all of the pieces, even without looking at them, their chess confidence can soar.

Continue on with the lessons, playing the naming game in-between lessons to help your child really get the names down. You don't need to wait until they can perfectly name all the pieces from memory before moving on.

The Chessboard

Now is a good time to introduce the chessboard.

Parents can forget to orient the child to the board. A chessboard can be overwhelming to a small child, so it is good to play some games to help them get used to it.

It is wise to avoid getting into how many squares there are on a board or how many rows there are. Neither is important at this stage and it doesn't help your child learn to play chess.

Older children will get oriented to the board through the piece movement drills later in this book, but younger children need more work on this point.

Step 1: This is a square!
Start by bringing out the board and laying it in front of your child.

If your child knows shapes, point to a square and ask them, "What shape is this?" If they don't know shapes, tell them, "This is called a square." Have them say it. They'll learn the new word. Point to two or three other squares, asking them to tell you what it is each time.

Step 2: These are white, black, dark, and light
Tell your child that there are white pieces and black pieces in chess. The white pieces that you have might in fact be cream or yellow. Explain that they are still called "white."

Point to a black piece and ask, "What color is this?" Then do the same with a white piece. Make sure they can identify a black piece and a white one.

Next point to a light square on the chessboard and explain, "This is a light square." Have them repeat it. Then point to a dark one and let them know it is a "dark square." It is best to teach them this early, so that they know the proper terms early.

Now point to a square and ask, "Is this light or dark?" Then another and another, asking, "How about this one?" This usually is a quick drill, just to help them learn these new terms.

Step 3: This is the center of a square
Point to the center of a square and tell them, "This is the center of a square." Do this a few times.

Now ask them to point to the center of a square. Have them do this several times, until you see that they can do this easily. If they point to a spot that isn't the center, simply show them more spots that are in the center.

Next put a piece in the center of a square, letting your child know that that's what you're doing. Then move the piece toward the edge of the square, while explaining that the piece should not go on the edges of the square. Then move it back to the center. You can repeat that the piece should be in the center.

Then explain that a piece isn't placed on the corner of the square, and move it to the corner, showing them how that would look. Make sure to put it back in the center of the square when you are done, explaining that this is where pieces go on a chessboard.

Next, quiz them on various points within a square, asking them, "Is this the center of the square?" Start with spots that are in the center and then point to obvious spots that aren't. Don't pick things that are in-between.

When they have this down, put a piece in the center of a square and tell them, "I'm putting this knight in the center of the square." Keep it there so that they have it as an example. Pick up another piece and ask them to place it in the center of a square too.

Do this with a few pieces, until you see that they can put a piece in the center of a square.

Coach's Corner

Silly questions can work!

When I ask a question and want my student to correctly answer, "no," I'll say it in a silly way. For instance I might say, "Is this the center of a square?" in a voice that very clearly says that it isn't. I exaggerate it, sometimes rolling my eyes as if it were the silliest thing ever. They giggle and say, "No!"

— Laura

Step 4: Pick a piece to put on the board
Now we're going to put some of these skills together.

Ask your child to ask you for a piece, making sure to include whether it is black or white. When they ask you for a certain piece, pull it out of the bag or box. Place it on the board in the center of a square, explaining that you are placing it in the center of the square.

Have your child ask for another piece. This time give them the piece and ask them to put it in the center of a square. Tell them that they can pick the square.

You want to discourage them from placing two pieces on one square, placing a piece on the corner of a square, or placing pieces on top of each other, as these things are never done in a chess game.

If they catch on to this quickly, add in the color of the square where you'd like them to place the piece. For instance, you might say, "Please put this one on a dark square."

Keep running through this exercise until all the pieces are on the board. Now ask them for a piece. "May I have a black pawn?" They may hand it to you or put it back in the bag. This is usually a popular end to this game.

Note: Some children will have an easy time with this, others will not. You can always help them with this by showing them more examples of correctly placing the piece on the square.

Step 5: Put that piece on the board
This is a different version of the game in step 4.

Place all the pieces by the side of the board. Ask your child to pick up a certain piece and place it on a light or dark square.

If they have trouble picking the right piece, you can point to it, but otherwise let them pick up the piece on their own. Continue to do this until each piece is on the board.

Once they have these exercises down, you can move on to piece movement. Some children will be ready immediately, while others may need to wait.

If they can listen to directions and copy your movements, they are ready to try. You will see very quickly whether they are ready or not. Typically, a child who isn't will move the rook, the first piece discussed, in giant circles around the board.

If that happens, just wait (perhaps a few months) and try again. One day, things will just pop into place and they will be able to move the pieces under your direction.

Speed

With these exercises it's important for you to keep the action moving along at a good speed. For instance if you're on Step 5: Put that piece on the board, you can tell them "Well done" when they've selected the right piece and be ready to request the next piece just as they are placing the old one in your hand.

If you wait too long, your child's attention will wander and you'll lose them.

Keep up the pace and they will rise to the challenge and really get into this exercise.

 **Troubleshooting Tips**

Problem:
My child can't name all the pieces in the Naming Game.

Solution:

This exercise can take time. However, if you notice that your child is having a lot of trouble with it, try playing the game with the pieces in view first.

If your child consistently misses one when the pieces are visible, spend a little time talking about that piece. Make up a game which really encourages them to use or talk about that piece in particular.

In the end, it isn't absolutely vital that they be able to name all the pieces without looking at them, but if you can get your child to do so, it is beneficial.

Coffee Talk

Understanding the words

One child seemed to suddenly lose interest in chess. It turned out that no one in his family ever read fairy tales, so the concept of a queen and king were foreign to him. Once we showed him picture books with queens and kings, he loved chess again.

Two years later, he's still enthusiastic about the game!

Problem:

My child is begging me to learn about the other pieces, but the lesson is going long.

Solution:

It is best to end the lesson with them wanting more. If you give in and go too long, you'll find their enthusiasm will decrease quickly. Then you could run into an uncomfortable situation of needing to end the lesson when they aren't enjoying it anymore.

Problem:

My child wants to know about the knight, but we're on the bishop.

Solution:

This can happen if they see all the pieces. Because the knight looks like a horse, children usually like it the best.

The solution to this problem is to not show them the pieces until you are ready to go over them. Keep them in the bag and only bring out the pieces you want to go over.

If they have seen the pieces, then you can change the order of the pieces and show them the knight. The order at this stage isn't crucial.

It's important not to overload them with names, though. For the first lesson, stick with two pieces and then stop.

Problem:
My child doesn't want to repeat the name of the piece.

Solution:
Don't force the issue. There are other ways to encourage them to name the pieces. In the beginning you can ask, "Is this a rook?"

When you get to the bishop, see if they will say "bishop." It could be that they are having trouble with the word "rook," especially if they are just learning to speak. However, if they won't say the word "bishop" either, it could be that they feel pressured.

Play a game that doesn't demand that they tell you the name of the piece. Give them all four rooks and bishops and ask them to give you a rook and then give you a bishop. If they are able to do that, try asking them to ask you for a piece. They may be willing to ask you for a rook at this point.

When they do say the piece's name, don't correct their pronunciation. Just continue to say the word correctly and praise them for getting it right.

If they still don't want to say the name, find other ways to do these exercises with them (like having them point to a queen or pick up a bishop, etc.).

Problem:
Yesterday when we ended the lesson, my child could name the rook and bishop, but today he has forgotten these pieces.

Solution:
It is important to do a rapid review of the last lesson. If the last lesson was long ago, you might have to start at the beginning, repeating all the steps. However, it should go faster, since you're reviewing.

Problem:
My child insists on calling the pieces by other names.

Solution:
Continue to use the correct words for the pieces and they should eventually follow along. You can correct them on occasion, but mostly ignore the other name and just use the right one.

Problem:
The chess set we have is confusing for my child.

Solution:
Buy a new set. They are $20 online (board, pieces, and bag). It is a good investment in your child's chess education. If you need help finding a set, please refer to www.ChessIsChildsPlay.com. We will provide you with options.

Problem:
My child likes to stack pieces on top of each other. Is this okay?

Solution:
Most children enjoy making a tall tower with chess pieces. It's fine to let them do this from time to time, but it should be after the lesson. Encourage them to play the games in this chapter. After the lesson is over, you can help them make a super tall tower!

Problem:
My child will not put the piece in the center of the square.

Solution:
Go back over "This is the center of a square" and make sure that your child understands what the center is. If they do, you can make a game of finding the center of other things. Have them point to the center of their favorite plate or move their body to the center of the room.

Then try asking them again to place a piece in the center of a square. If your child insists on putting the piece on the corner or edge of a square, it's a good idea to wait a bit before continuing with the chess lessons. They need to be able to follow your directions regarding putting a piece in the center of a square to continue.

If you do wait a few months, make sure to start back at the beginning of the drills and review each step.

Problem:
My child is very happy playing these games. Should I move on to the next chapter?

Solution:
You may continue to play these games as long as you like. Keep in mind that we introduce piece movement in the same, gentle way, so chances are your child is ready for this step.

If you venture forward and realize that they are not ready, feel free to come back to these introductory games for a while.

The Rook

5

he rook is the best piece to start with when teaching a child. Its movement is simple, so it's the easiest to master.

When teaching your child, make sure to use your board and pieces. Don't show them this book's diagrams, as the diagrams may confuse your child and slow their speed of learning.

It's a good idea for you to read this chapter all the way through first, so you know all the steps. You can also practice the exercises, so that you know them well, before you sit down with your child.

Throughout this book, we will be using diagrams to show you how to set up a chessboard. We will always have White placed at the bottom of the board, and Black at the top.

Step 1: Put a rook on the board
Set up your board with the rook in the middle.

Just these little facts:

1. The child knows they see a rook. They know it's called a rook.

2. They see one rook all by itself on the chessboard, so it looks fairly simple.

3. They realize they're going to learn how the pieces move.

…these little facts can generate lots of excitement for a child (and an adult)!

One of our purposes is to help keep that fire burning brightly for every child who wants to learn the game.

— Bill

Diagram 5.1

1a. Tell your child how the rook moves: Tell your child that a rook can move forwards, backwards, or side to side.

Point to all the squares where the rook can go.

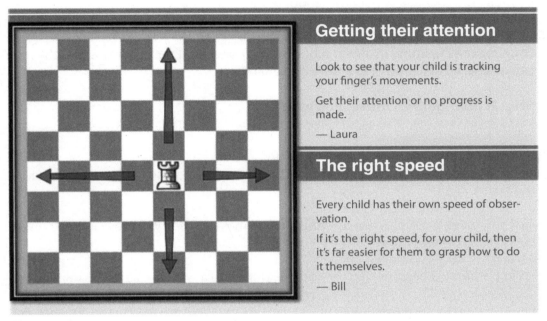

Diagram 5.2

It can be helpful to start by pointing to each square to which the rook can move. Then, as your child gets used to seeing the piece on the board, you may speed up this process by tracing a line with your finger.

Either way, it is important not to spend too much time on this step, or you can lose your child's interest.

1b. Parent – I move the rook: Show your child how to move a rook. Make one rook move. Then let go of the piece. Then move the rook again and let go. While you are moving the piece, explain what you're doing.

Avoid using the words "right" and "left," because these terms can be confusing. Keep in mind that while "forward" and "backward" are better, they can still be unclear (what is forwards to you is backwards to them).

You might say something like, "See, I'm moving the rook sideways. Now I'm moving this way."

Make a few different moves with the rook, making sure to move it in all the directions possible. You should also vary the length of the move (move the rook one square, then move it a few squares, and then move it all the way across the board).

Once the rook is sitting in a new spot, you can point to all the squares where the rook can go again. Then move it to a few new squares.

Step 2: Mini-game: I move, you move

This is the first mini-game!

Here's how it works. Using only one rook, take turns with your child moving it around the board.

First you move the rook. Then ask your child to move it. Then you move it and then ask your child to move it. Take turns back and forth.

It's important to keep this step very simple. Don't add anything else to this mini-game.

Pay attention to the moves your child makes. Encourage them to vary the direction and the number of squares they move the rook, making sure you do the same when it is your turn.

If they need some help, you can point in the direction you'd like them to move the rook, saying, "you can move it that way" or, "you could move it this way."

Give your child guidance. You can point or drag your finger along the center of the line of squares they could move.

The focus here is to teach them to move it correctly, to a square where the rook could go.

If they still have trouble or are hesitant, you can point to a specific square where the rook can go and ask them to move it there. They will learn by doing the actions required to move the piece.

If you find that your child only moves the rook one square at a time, make a point of moving the rook two or three squares when it is your turn, telling them that you're doing so. Show by example how the rook can move different lengths.

This game is made more exciting by slightly increasing your speed. Start slow and when you see that they are more confident, move a bit faster. They will follow you and make their moves faster. Encourage this. You want them to pick up their speed to match yours.

If your child starts making mistakes, slow down and guide them to make correct moves. You can remind them how the rook moves by showing them a few correct moves.

When they can move the rook with you quickly and correctly, end the lesson and move on.

Coffee Talk

The importance of simplicity

One parent told us that he had started by teaching his young child to move the pawn. He quickly realized that he started at the wrong end.

The pawn is actually the most complicated piece. He had much more success starting with the rook.

Tip for younger children

When you are teaching a very young child, you will want to show them a lot of examples and then have them copy your moves to start. Move the rook one square, let go, and then put it back to where it started. Now have them do that same exact move.

Just getting the right form down may take some time. Keep going with it until they can do it easily. Copying your movements is often a fun game for them!

Remember to give a nice acknowledgement to them for doing it correctly.

Step 3: This is how you move a chess piece

Now that you have shown your child how a rook moves, it is time to show them the correct form to use when moving a piece.

When a child moves a chess piece, they should always:

1. Pick up the piece (making sure it doesn't go too high up from the board).
2. Place it in the center of the target square.
3. Let go of the piece.

These three steps are the basic form for moving any chess piece.

In the beginning your child may make basic errors in these steps. Here are some common errors:

- They land the piece on the edge of the square.
- They lift the piece way up off the board.
- They hop the piece along the board.
- They don't let go of the piece.

Gently correct these mistakes as they come up, making sure that you practice proper form when you move a piece.

Move the rook again, showing them how you are following correct form. Tell them that you are putting the piece in the center of the square.

Make sure to let it go before moving it again. Remember, you're teaching them that each move is its own move, different from the next.

Step 4: Mini-game: I move, you move with correct form

Make a move with the rook and have your child make a move. Watch for correct form. If they make one of the common errors, show them the correct way to move the piece.

For instance, if they shoot the piece straight up into the air before bringing it down to the board, explain that the piece shouldn't go too high, and show them the correct way to move the rook on your turn.

If they land the piece on the edge of a square, show them how the rook should move so that it lands in the center.

When they move the rook correctly, make a point of letting them know that they did it well. Keep alternating moves until they show you that they can move the rook with correct form.

Step 5: The rook can go here, the rook can't go there

You want to make sure your child understands that the rook cannot just go from any square to any other square on the board. It can't just move in any and every direction.

Now is a good time to go over incorrect moves.

Move the rook incorrectly, saying, "The rook cannot move like this." Now make a couple of correct moves and say, "The rook moves like this."

Keep doing this back and forth, mostly making correct moves, but always saying whether your move is correct or incorrect. This exercise shouldn't take long.

Step 6: Mini-game: Can the rook go here?

Start by making a move that you know the child knows is a correct rook move. Ask them, "Can the rook go here?"

Keep asking that question, moving the rook correctly. Then make a move that is obviously incorrect, asking, "Can the rook go here?" The first time you ask, it is fine to give them a hint that it isn't correct by asking in such a way that they know it isn't.

If they have any confusion, simply show them correct rook moves for a few turns. Then show them a few incorrect moves. Then ask them about the same incorrect move you quizzed them on.

As they get more and more answers correct, increase your speed and keep up the quizzing.

When they can get the answers correct at a fast speed (about five answers in 10 seconds), you can move on.

Step 7: Mini-game: I move, you move, 2 rooks

Set up this position:

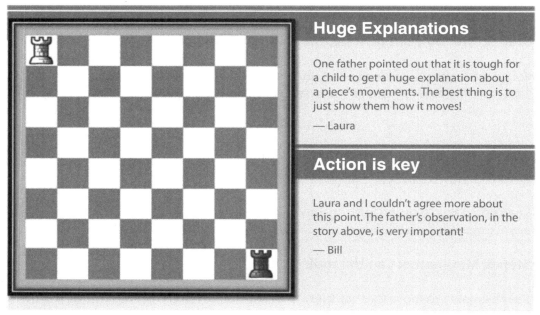

Huge Explanations

One father pointed out that it is tough for a child to get a huge explanation about a piece's movements. The best thing is to just show them how it moves!

— Laura

Action is key

Laura and I couldn't agree more about this point. The father's observation, in the story above, is very important!

— Bill

Diagram 5.3

You should take White for this game, so that you go first.

Explain that White always goes first. As before, you will take turns making moves.

In this mini-game, you are just giving them practice moving a rook, adding in the idea of alternating moves.

Avoid taking their rook at this stage, because we haven't covered that yet.

If your child moves their rook so that you can take their piece, move away. When it is your turn, make sure you don't put your rook in a position where it could be taken.

Keep making moves, faster and faster until it is clear that they have mastered the rook move. Of course, you want to make sure that they are varying the rook moves, not just moving it back and forth along the same path.

Coffee Talk

The Power Of Mini-Games

Kids love games. Each little part of chess is more fun to learn when you use the mini-games technique.

During one mini-game, a two-year-old girl set her toy dinosaurs along the side of the board, announcing to her father, "They want to watch us play!"

Troubleshooting Tips

Problem:
My child says she understands how to do the step, but she cannot actually do it correctly on the board.

Solution:
Children want to please you. They want to get the right answer and dislike making mistakes. Sometimes when they don't understand something they will still nod their head, saying they understand.

In chess, if they understand it, they can do it.

Here's the bottom line: If the child can't move the rook, if they really can't show you the move on the chessboard, then they didn't understand something about the piece's movement.

There's a big difference between won't do it, or doesn't want to do it, and can't do it. In chess, if they can't do it then there's something about it they do not yet understand. With correct teaching, they will get it.

Don't get impatient. If you see they can't do the exercise, it means that they haven't grasped an earlier step that you thought they learned, or that they haven't fully understood something about the current exercise.

You can have them use their own words and motions to describe how to move the rook, but make sure they aren't just giving your words or motions back to you, without understanding them. The way they describe the action may give you a clue as to which step they didn't actually understand.

For instance, if they say, "The rook always moves all the way down the board," you know that they think that the rook can't just move a few squares. In this case, you can give them lots of examples of how the rook can move.

The only real way to test their knowledge is to have them make movements with the rook. If they are unable to move the rook properly, they are missing something.

Problem:
My child tends to move the rook off the line it is on, curving it onto another square.

Solution:
It can be hard for a child to maintain the line all the way across the board, especially if they are very young.

To help them, start with shorter movements, one to three squares across the board. Then build up from there.

Also make sure that they can reach all the way across the board. Sometimes the problem is that their arms aren't long enough. The solution then is to use a lower table or play on the floor, so that their arms can reach further.

Problem:
When I ask my child to move the rook on his own, he always moves it one square at a time.

Solution:
Go back a step and have them copy your moves. Show them how the rook can move two squares, then three, etc.

You can also point to a square a few squares away and have them move it there. Then ask them to move the rook. It might take some practice and they might resist moving it more than one square at a time for a while. Just keep at it and show them by example that the rook can move longer distances.

Problem:
My child only moves the rook all the way across the board.

Solution:
Ask them if the rook can move only two or three squares. They will probably say yes. Ask them to show you.

You can also go back to having them copy your moves or pointing to squares, to give them the idea that the rook can move any number of squares.

Problem:
My child hops on each square, along the path it travels, when moving the rook.

Solution:
Explain that the rook doesn't need to touch each square on its path. Ask them if they can just move the rook to the end square. They will probably do it. It is good to rid them of the habit of hopping the rook on each square.

Problem:
My child doesn't put the piece in the center of the square.

Solution:
Check to see that they know where the center of the square is. To check this out, point to the center of a square and ask, "Is this the center of this square?" Ask a few more and then point to the edge of the square and ask the same question ("Is this the center of the square?").

Then have them point to the center of a few squares. Next, ask them to put the rook in the center of the square. Then have them move it to another square, landing it in the center.

Problem:
My child just moves the rook in circles.

Solution:
There are a few things you can try. See if you can get them to copy your rook movements. Make short movements (these are easiest for a child to do). Start by moving the rook only one square.

You can also print out a single line of checkered squares on the computer (you can find them online) and have your child practice moving the rook along the line.

They might not be ready to make chess moves. If this is the case, keep playing the games that involve putting the pieces on the board and naming them.

Problem:
My child is bored with chess and doesn't seem to like the game.

Solution:
This is rarely the actual situation. Most likely, you have just gone a little too quickly for your child or, in some instances, a bit too slowly. This is fixable.

If your child can show you easily that they can move the rook, move forward with the next lesson. If they aren't quite perfect with it, you can still move on. They'll keep learning about the rook as they go on. You're not seeking perfection with each step before advancing to the next.

If your child cannot move the rook correctly or often moves it incorrectly, they are missing a step. The solution is to review the earlier steps.

Also, review the tips. For instance, make sure that your child isn't hungry or tired. And keep the lessons short. Remember it is always best to end the lesson when they still want more.

Problem:
My child doesn't want to do all the drills but would like to play a complete game already.

Solution:
If you make the mini-games challenging and fun, and play them at the right speed, your child will have a blast. Your attitude is important – you need to know that this is the correct way to teach kids chess.

If you were to race through the piece-movement chapters, teaching them all the pieces in one sitting, they could set up the board and "play." However they will get lost quickly, feeling very overwhelmed.

The solution would now be to go back through these drills more slowly. It's easier to just do that right from the start.

How to Take
THE OTHER PLAYER'S CHESS PIECES

6

ow that your child has learned how to move the rook, you'll show them how they can capture a piece from the other player. This is an exciting step for most children!

Correct Form

When a child first tries to take the other player's piece, they often pick up their piece and the opponent's piece, taking them both off the board. The problem with this technique is that they then usually forget where the two pieces were.

The solution is to teach them the correct form right from the start.

There are two basic ways that you can take a piece. The first one is the most common for young students, as their hands are smaller. The second one given is for older children.

The "Slide & Nudge" Technique

Here are the steps involved with the "slide and nudge" technique:

1. Slide the white rook over to the black rook.
2. Nudge the black rook out of the center of its square with the white rook, until the white rook is now occupying the center.
3. Let go of the white rook.
4. Pick up the black rook with the same hand.
5. Place the black rook off the board, to the side.

Perform each step slowly, allowing them time to get used to the technique.

The One-Hand Pickup

Here are the steps involved with the "one-hand pick-up" technique (used by older children and adults):

1. Pick up the white rook with the thumb and forefinger.
2. Bring it over to the black rook.
3. Using the same hand, pick up the black rook with the free fingers (still holding

the white rook).

4. Tilt your hand, placing the white rook onto the square (still holding the black rook).

5. Let go of the white rook and place the black rook off the board.

Although a very young child could be taught the "one-hand pickup" technique, it would take far too much time. Plus, the complicated hand motion can be frustrating for them.

The "slide and nudge" technique is much easier and is perfectly acceptable until they can master the "one-hand pickup" technique.

Regardless of which technique is used, discourage your child from using two hands to take another player's piece. Simple teach them to do it all with one hand.

Step 1: Here's How You Take the Other Player's Piece

Set up this position:

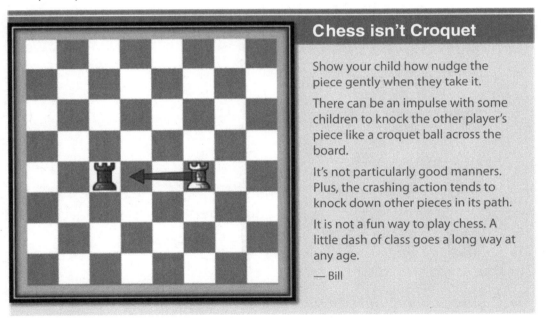

Chess isn't Croquet

Show your child how nudge the piece gently when they take it.

There can be an impulse with some children to knock the other player's piece like a croquet ball across the board.

It's not particularly good manners. Plus, the crashing action tends to knock down other pieces in its path.

It is not a fun way to play chess. A little dash of class goes a long way at any age.

— Bill

Diagram 6.1

1a: I take the rook

Tell your child that the white rook can take the black rook, because it is on the path of the white rook. Since the rook can move to that square, it can take the piece that is in its way.

Show them how it is done, using the piece-taking technique you feel they can master.

By the way, the word "opponent" is a mouthful. We use "other player" with success.

1b: You take the rook
Now reset the position above and have your child take the black rook. It might take a few tries to get the correct form down, but once they learn it, it gets much easier.

Don't let them struggle with the "one-hand pickup." The "slide and nudge" technique is perfectly acceptable.

1c: You take the white rook
Now reset the position and point out that the black rook can take the white rook, if it was Black's turn. Have your child take the white rook, using the same technique used in 1b.

Step 2: Mini-Game: I Take, You Take, One Rook
Set up a different position:

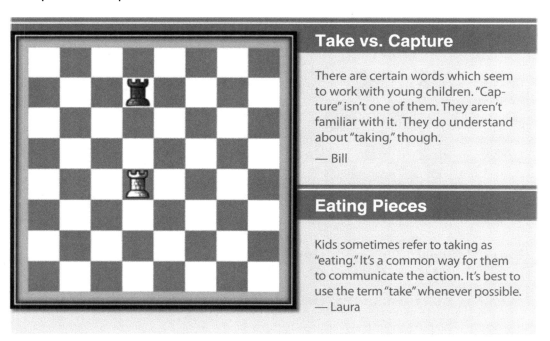

Take vs. Capture

There are certain words which seem to work with young children. "Capture" isn't one of them. They aren't familiar with it. They do understand about "taking," though.

— Bill

Eating Pieces

Kids sometimes refer to taking as "eating." It's a common way for them to communicate the action. It's best to use the term "take" whenever possible.
— Laura

Diagram 6.2

Start by showing your child how the black rook takes the white rook. Then reset the position and have them take the black rook with the white rook.

Now set up different position, moving the rooks a little farther away. Take one rook and then have them take the other. If they have trouble with this task, then set up a position where the rooks are closer.

When your child can use the proper form to take a rook, you can move on.

Step 3: Mini-Game: Can You Take My Rook?

Now that your child knows that one piece can take another, it is important to quiz them on when this can happen.

Set up the board in a position where one rook can take the other. Tell your child to pretend that they are playing Black. Ask, "Can you take my rook?"

If they say no, work out with them all the places where the rook can go. This will help them see that they can take the white rook.

If they say yes, move the white rook to another square, where Black could take it. Ask "Can you take my rook?" again. Keep this up and then put the white rook on a square where the black rook cannot take it. Ask the same question.

If your child says yes, review with them how the rook moves. Then you can ask them to point to all the squares where the rook can move. Help them see that the black rook can't take the white one. Move the white rook around the board to different squares, asking if they can take it with their rook.

Now switch colors and tell your child that they are playing White. Move the black rook around the board asking the same question, "Can you take my rook?" Increase the speed as they answer correctly.

Step 4: Mini-Game: I Move, You Move, With Taking

Set up this position:

Normally the rooks would all begin in

Diagram 6.3

the corners, but in this case we adjusted their starting positions, so that no piece can be taken on the first move.

Now there can be a "winner" and "loser" but that shouldn't be the focus of this mini-game. The goal is to make a game of noticing when pieces can be taken, and using proper form to do so.

After a few moves, put your rook in danger. If they don't see that they can take your rook, give them a hint by asking, "Can you take my rook?" Give them a chance to find the move, but if they can't, help them.

If they put their rook in danger, let them know by saying, "If you move your rook there, can I take it?" Give them a chance to move out of danger. They are liable to become discouraged if they lose their rook too quickly.

If either side loses both rooks, set up the same mini-game and play again. Once your child gets the hang of this mini-game and doesn't lose their rooks, go on to the next step.

Step 5: It's Okay to Trade Pieces

Explain to your child that sometimes they might take the other player's rook and then the other player will take their rook. This is called a "trade."

Pick up a black rook and hand them a white rook. Explain that since you have each gotten a rook, it's an even trade.

It can be upsetting to a young player to lose a piece, especially if they don't understand that trading "a rook for a rook" is fine. Another way of wording it is, "giving up your rook but also getting their rook." Trading is an important part of chess.

Now show them how this might come up in the mini-game. Here's an example:

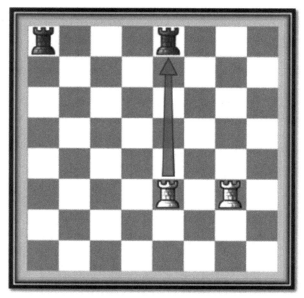

Diagram 6.4

Now if White takes Black's rook, it will look like this:

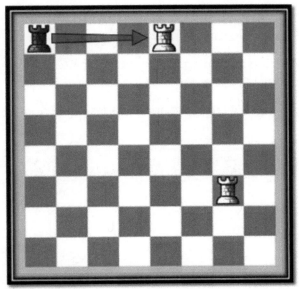

Diagram 6.5

And then if Black takes back, it will look like this:

Diagram 6.6

At the end of the sequence of moves, each player gets a rook from the other player. This is an even trade.

Set up a few positions like this, so that your child can see how trades work.

Now play another mini-game or two, focusing on trading. See if you can create positions where your rook can take back theirs if they take you.

Don't worry too much if it doesn't come up. We'll talk more about trades later.

Troubleshooting Tips

Problem:
My child tends to take both pieces off the board when capturing.

Solution:
Most likely this is because your child is using two hands. It is difficult to do this with one hand.

Show them the "slide and nudge" technique again. This time, when you do it, sit on your free hand. Make sure they see that.

Now ask them to sit on their free hand and use the "slide and nudge" technique. This technique does take practice, as it is common for children to want to use two hands.

Problem:
My child sees me using the "one-hand pickup" technique and really wants to use that system, too, but is having trouble.

Solution:
Make sure you are using the same technique that your child is learning. If you're using the one-hand pickup technique, they will want to do that too. It's natural. They want to play just like you do.

For now, use the "slide and nudge" system, until they can handle the other.

Problem:
My child gets upset when he loses.

Solution:

The focus on these mini-games shouldn't be winning or losing. It is really about learning the correct form of taking the other player's pieces.

For now, try to keep the rooks in play even. If your child moves so that you can take their rook, give them a chance to move out of danger.

Problem:

My child isn't moving the rook correctly.

Solution:

It is to be expected that they might make an occasional error in moving the rook. This is because they are focusing on other elements now and the rook's movement is still new to them.

However, if they are consistently moving the rook incorrectly, take some time to show them examples of correct rook moves. Play the "I move, you move" mini-game (with one rook) to give them more practice.

The Bishop

7

T he next piece to teach, after the rook, is the bishop. It introduces the concept of diagonals.

Defining Diagonal

The word "diagonal" is not always completely understood by young students.

Step 1: Explain what a diagonal is

Although you will show them what a diagonal is on the chessboard, you can also help them to understand the concept by using your arms.

Here is a good explanation: Hold one arm straight up and say, "This arm goes up," and then hold one arm sideways right next to it, and say, "This arm goes sideways." Then move the arm which is up, down until it is slanted and say, "Now this is diagonal."

Then you can also make an "X" with your two arms, explaining that these are two diagonals. Also, the letter "X" is familiar to most children at an early age. Each line of the "X" is a diagonal.

Throughout your chess lessons you will use this word a lot, so it is important to help your child fully understand it. You may need to refresh their memory on this term.

If it gets too confusing, you can skip the word altogether for a while. You can say that the bishop moves on a slant. Your child can learn the way the bishop moves, the action of moving the bishop on a diagonal without knowing the word diagonal or slant.

With demonstration from you and practice involving their own observation and actions, they will be able to move the bishop properly along the diagonals.

In a nutshell, the word "diagonal" does not have to be a hindrance to the action of moving bishops along diagonals, but the word is valuable if they understand it.

Step 2: Here's how a bishop moves

Set up your board with the bishop in the center of the board.

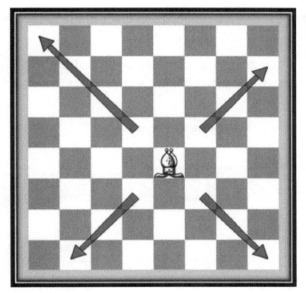

2a. Tell your child how it moves:
Explain to your child that a bishop moves diagonally.

Diagram 7.1

2b. I point to the squares:
Point to all the squares where the bishop can go from this center square. Hit all squares on all diagonals.

Make sure to point them out at an appropriate speed in order to keep your child's interest. You can combine the technique of pointing to all the squares and dragging your finger along the diagonals.

2c. I move the bishop:
Move your bishop along one of the diagonals. It is a good idea to start with a short move (maybe two or three squares away).

Then, after letting go of the piece, pick up the bishop and move it across one of the other diagonals, maybe one square. Tell your child what you are doing with each step.

Continue to vary the direction and length of the moves, so that they see what they can do with the bishop.

After you have moved the bishop a few times, point to the squares again, showing where the bishop can move.

Step 3: Mini-game: I move, you move
In this mini-game you will alternate moves with your child, using one bishop. You make the first move. Then ask them to move the bishop.

If they are uncertain or hesitant about where to go, you can make a suggestion. Point to a square a short distance away. The longer the distance, the harder it is for them to make a correct movement.

When they have made a few correct moves, move on to the next step.

Coffee Talk

Tiles

A five-year-old boy was taking a bath one evening. His mother was surprised when he looked up at the tiles and showed her the bishop's moves.

Later he started walking like a bishop on the kitchen tiles!

Step 4: The bishop can move like this, it can't move like that
Make some correct moves with the bishop. Then throw in a few that aren't right. For instance, move the bishop forward three squares and say, "The bishop cannot move like this."

Make a few more correct and incorrect moves.

Step 5: Mini-game: Can the bishop go here?
Make various moves with the bishop and ask your child, "Can the bishop go here?" Make the first few correct moves and then move the bishop forward a few squares, asking the same question.

Start slowly and if your child has any confusion, show them a few correct moves and a few incorrect moves. If they continue to hesitate, go back to the "I move, you move" mini-game.

When your child can confidently tell you when the bishop can move to the squares you point to, speed up the game. Move the bishop as fast as you can and see if they keep up with you. Vary the question to match the faster speed. You may ask, "Can the bishop go here? How about here? And here?"

When they really have it, they should be able to get about 10 correct answers (with no mistakes and no hesitation) in about 20 seconds.

Step 6: There are two kinds of bishops in chess

Explain to your child that in chess you have two bishops. One of the bishops moves only on the light-colored squares and is called a "light-squared" bishop.

The other bishop moves on the dark squares and is called a "dark-squared" bishop.

Place a black light-squared bishop and a white dark-squared bishop on the board. Play a few moves of "I move, you move" with the two bishops.

Move your bishop next to theirs, so that they can see the point that you are about to discuss with them.

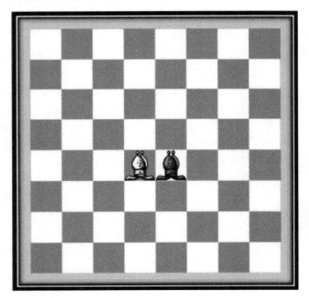

Your child may try to take your bishop, momentarily forgetting that the bishops can't move sideways. If so, do a quick review on how the bishop moves and then play a few more moves of this mini-game.

Now talk to your child about how, in this mini-game, neither bishop can take the other. Discuss it with them and have them really look at how this is true. This is a surprise for most beginners.

Diagram 7.2

Have them look at where the two bishops can go. Help them see that the dark-squared bishop can never go on the light squares and the light-squared bishop can never go on the dark squares.

Keep playing this mini-game until your child really sees this point.

Enthusiasm Spreads Fast

One mother told me that her three-year-old daughter couldn't stop talking about chess after school.

She had just mastered the bishop move and wanted to share her new-found knowledge with her mother.

Step 7: Mini-game: I move, you move with rooks and bishops

Set up this position:

As with most of these mini-games, White goes first.

At first, many children mix up the bishop's and the rook's movements. This exercise isolates these pieces and gives them practice mastering these two piece movements.

Diagram 7.3

The only focus of this mini-game is piece movement. It is fine if they want to take your pieces, but try to avoid taking theirs (or putting yours in danger) for now.

In the next chapter, "Attacking and Protecting," we will revisit this mini-game.

Problem:

My child doesn't move the bishop along a path, but curves it on the board or moves it along another line.

Solution:

First make sure that they can comfortably reach across the table. If their arms are too short, it might be impossible for them to reach the correct square.

If they have no trouble reaching the far side of the board, have them point to all the squares where a bishop can go along a diagonal. Have them do this with the bishop in different positions (for instance, put the bishop in the middle of the board, close to the edge, on the edge, and in the corner).

Then play "I move, you move," but use shorter bishop movements.

Give them a chance to master moving the bishop correctly two or three squares. Then encourage them to go four squares and have them play with that a bit. Gradually build up to the point where they can go five, six, or seven squares.

You may need to place your finger on the square where the bishop will end up. It is also a very good idea to have them copy your movements. Typically, the younger the child, the more difficult this piece is to master.

Problem:

My child can move the bishop, but cannot do it quickly.

Solution:

Practice more. Work at the speed that they can do and then slowly increase it. Make sure to observe what they can do and stick to that speed.

Sometimes a child will continually look up at you for approval. This is a habit you should gently discourage. If they look up at you questioningly, ask, "What do you think? Is that right?" Try not to nod your approval with each guess.

It's important that they are confident with the bishop's movement before moving on to the next piece. Although they will continue to practice each piece's movement throughout the book, it is best that they feel comfortable with the diagonal movement now.

Problem:

My child gets the answers to the mini-games right most of the time, but sometimes makes mistakes.

Solution:

Be observant. Pay attention to the simplest of actions that they are trying to do. You'll soon discover why they are making these mistakes. If they tend to get it right, but make occasional slips, there could be a variety of reasons.

For instance, if they are hungry or tired, it will be harder for them to get any chess exercise down perfectly.

If they consistently make the same errors, that is very different from making occasional errors. When moves are consistently incorrect, find the earlier mini-game that will help them with the most basic skill they can't do.

For instance, if they are having trouble with "Can the bishop go here?" then go back to "I move, you move," continuing with that mini-game until they can move the bishop quickly.

If your child makes an error and instantly corrects it, continue with the exercise. They are just building their confidence and practicing the skill.

Problem:

My child wants to move the bishop like a rook.

Solution:

It is common for children to confuse these two pieces. It takes some practice to get it down. Show them examples of both piece movements and practice the "I move, you move" mini-game.

Coach's Corner

Dogs Can't Fly

Ask your child how a bird moves. Then ask how a dog moves. They'll see that the two animals move differently.

Explain that chess pieces also have their own movements. Dogs can't fly and a bishop can't move like a rook.

How to Attack
AND DEFEND PIECES

8

y now your child has noticed that their pieces can be attacked and taken.

Most children do not immediately realize they can move a piece to a square where it threatens to take a piece. Learning this simple and powerful move, "an attack," is the next step.

Step 1: Let's attack the rook

Set up this position:

Taking pieces is fun!

In the beginning when a child's pieces are taken, they usually don't like it.

When they see that they can take the other player's piece, they love it!

— Bill

Diagram 8.1

Tell your child that there is a square where the bishop can go where it will attack the rook. Work with your child to try to find that square.

Start by seeing if they can find it immediately. Some will. If not, one approach is to have them point to all the squares where the bishop can go. For each square, have your child check to see if the bishop attacks the rook.

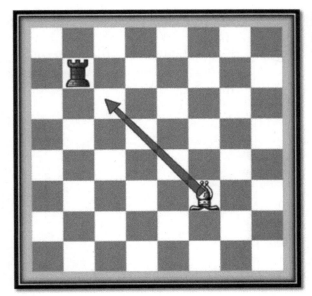

If they have trouble finding the square, move the bishop to show them the attacking diagonal.

Diagram 8.2

Set up a few more positions and allow your child to figure out how to move their piece to attack the other player.

Sometimes there will be two correct answers, as in diagram 8.3:

Diagram 8.3

Ask your child to move the bishop, so that it attacks the black rook. Then see if your child can find the other square, where the bishop can move to attack the rook.

Diagram 8.4

Step 2: Now let's attack the bishop

Set up this position:

Ask your child to move the rook, so that it can attack the bishop.

Diagram 8.5

Now have your child find the other square where the rook can attack the bishop.

Note: These two squares are marked on diagram 8.6.

Set up more positions like this.

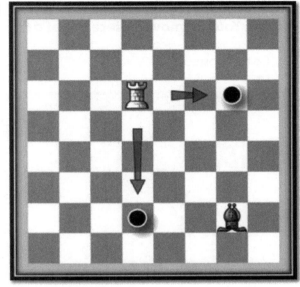

Diagram 8.6

Step 3: Pieces can attack each other

Now set up this position again:

Point out to your child that, depending on whose turn it is, the rook could attack the bishop or the bishop could attack the rook.

This opens the door to the idea that not only can you attack the other player's pieces, but they can also attack yours.

Have your child point out all the ways the pieces can attack each other.

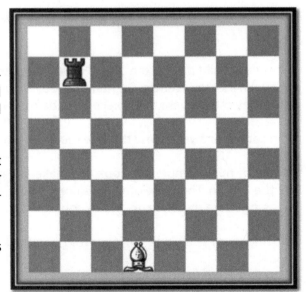

Diagram 8.7

Set up another position like this. Remember to use only the rook and bishop, because these are the pieces that your child knows at this stage.

Step 4: You can move a piece out of danger

Set up this position:

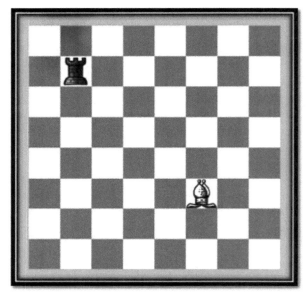

Diagram 8.8

After your child has gotten Step 3 down, you can teach them how to get a piece out of danger. After you set up diagram 8.8, point out that their piece is attacked. Ask them how they can prevent their piece from being taken.

The correct answer here is that the rook must move.

Note: In this example, the rook can make any move and it will no longer be attacked by the bishop. There are other positions where the rook would need to watch where it goes, but here there are no unsafe squares.

Moving away is a good way to avoid an attack. We'll go over other ways later in this book.

Set up a few more positions like this and ask your child to get the rook out of danger.

Now set up this position:

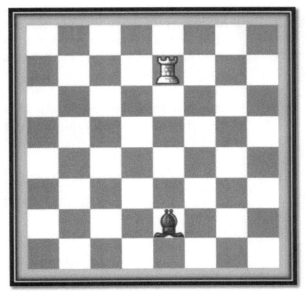

Ask your child how they can get the black bishop out of danger. Again, with this position, any move that the bishop makes will get it out of danger.

Diagram 8.9

As a next step you can set up this position:

Diagram 8.10

Now there is one move that the bishop could make that would not get it out of danger. If it moves to the spot indicated in diagram 8.11, it could still be taken.

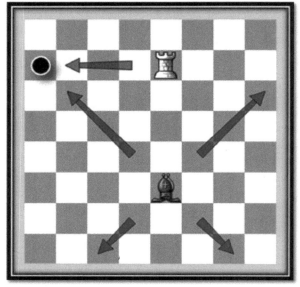

Make sure to point this out to your child and get them to see that they need to make sure that the piece is safe in the new square.

Set up more examples like this and quiz your child on how they can get out of danger.

Diagram 8.11

Step 5: Pieces can attack each other at the same time

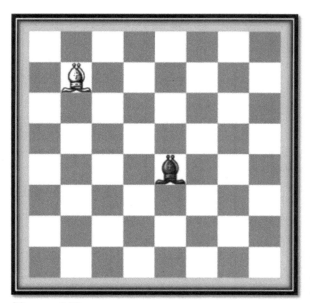

Here, in diagram 8.12, the white bishop is attacking the black bishop and vice versa. It depends on whose turn it is. If it's White's turn, White can take Black's bishop. If it's Black's turn, Black can take White.

It's good to point this out because it is trickier to attack a piece that can attack you back, as those are times you move directly into attack as soon as you attack.

Show your child a few examples of this with "bishop moving to attack bishop" and then with "rook moving to attack rook."

Diagram 8.12

Defining support

When one piece supports another it means that it can take back the attacker, after the attacker takes a piece.

Step 6: One piece can support another

In Step 4 we talked about how a piece can move to handle the attack. Another way to get out of danger is to support your piece with another piece. Set up this example:

Diagram 8.13

In diagram 8.13, the rooks are supporting the bishops.

If it were Black's turn, Black could take the white bishop and the white rook would take back.

Or if it were White's turn, the white bishop could take the black one and the black rook could take back White's bishop.

Diagram 8.14

Set up more examples like this, showing how one piece can support another.

Step 7: Mini-game: Attacking and protecting

Set up this position:

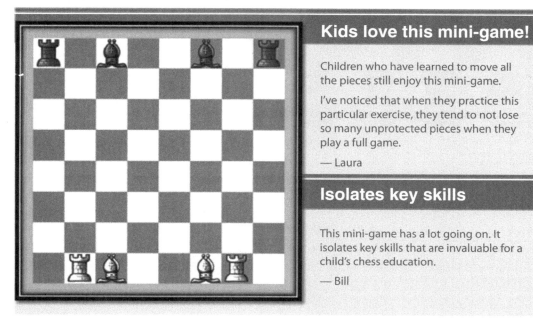

Kids love this mini-game!

Children who have learned to move all the pieces still enjoy this mini-game.

I've noticed that when they practice this particular exercise, they tend to not lose so many unprotected pieces when they play a full game.

— Laura

Isolates key skills

This mini-game has a lot going on. It isolates key skills that are invaluable for a child's chess education.

— Bill

Diagram 8.15

Even though there are just two types of pieces on the board, this mini-game is rich with possibilities! Your child will learn to notice when they can take a piece and when their piece can be taken.

Ask questions like, "Can you attack my rook?" to help them. Or, "Can you find a piece that I'm attacking?" when you move your piece so that it is attacking one of theirs.

Step 8: Rooks are worth more than bishops

In chess, the different pieces have different values. Some are worth more than others.

Set up this position:

Show your child that here White can take Black's bishop.

Diagram 8.16

And then Black can take the white bishop.

Diagram 8.17

Diagram 8.18

Show your child that you've just traded a bishop for a bishop. If they take your bishop and you take their bishop, it's an even trade.

Now explain that the rook is usually worth more than the bishop. The rook can usually do more and is more powerful, so it is worth more to a player. For one thing, the rook can go on both dark squares and light squares, while the bishop can't.

Show your child trades that wouldn't be good. Set up this position:

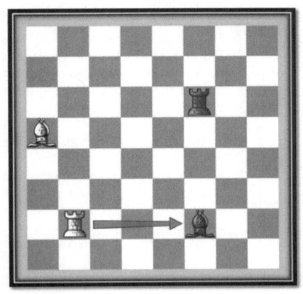

Diagram 8.19

Here White can take the black bishop, but is that a good move?

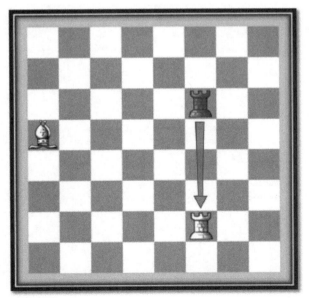

Diagram 8.20

Show your child how it would play out:

Here White took the black bishop.

Diagram 8.21

And Black took the white rook. Show your child the pieces that were removed from the board. White got a bishop and Black got a rook. Who got the better trade?

Show your child more examples like this and then quiz them on various positions, showing trades, asking them if they would make the trade or not.

In the Chapter "The Value of the Pieces," we will discuss which pieces are worth more or less, compared to others. For right now, just keep things simple. Don't discuss the values of other pieces. Emphasize that a rook is worth more than a bishop.

Step 9: Mini-game: Attacking and protecting considering piece value

Set up this position again:

Diagram 8.22

Play this mini-game with your child, making sure they see when a trade is good for them and when it isn't.

This mini-game can be played a lot, with great benefit for your child. Make sure that they attack you, support their pieces, make good trades, and know when to move their pieces out of danger.

Coffee Talk

Again and again

One mother was amazed at how much her son loved the "Attacking and Protecting" mini-game. He wanted to play it again and again. She said he started really creating plans of attack, thinking in terms of future moves.

Troubleshooting Tips

Problem:
My child has trouble seeing how to attack the other player's piece.

Solution:
If they're having trouble with this, start by showing them a number of examples. Make sure you're only using two pieces at a time. Set up positions with a rook and bishop and then show them how the bishop can attack the rook.

After you have shown them a few examples, give them a similar position (if not the same one you just showed them) and ask them to attack the rook.

Of course you'll want to make sure your child has no difficulty moving the bishop and the rook. If they don't understand about diagonal movement, this exercise will be difficult.

Problem:
My child moves her piece where I can take it.

Solution:
This aspect of the game takes some practice. In the beginning, don't take the offered piece. Rather, tell your child that their piece can be taken.

Make sure to show your child how you can take their piece. Sometimes that is all that is needed to train you child to notice when their pieces are attacked and can be taken.

If they continue to put their pieces in danger, have them point to the squares where your pieces can go, until they notice that their piece can be taken. A skilled chess player can see all the squares where all the pieces can go very quickly, but for a beginner this skill can take time.

It is also a good idea to suggest ways that they can support an attacked piece.

You can also take the piece from time to time, to show them that their pieces can be taken if they don't watch out. Take it and then offer to let them take back the move.

Problem:
My child makes moves without looking at my moves.

Solution:
Watch for this, as it is a common habit with beginners. They get so wrapped up in their moves and their ideas that they forget to look at the other player's moves.

If you see that your child's eyes aren't tracking with your move, ask them, "What was my last move?" If they weren't paying attention to your move, that may startle them a bit.

Show them your move. If you were attacking one of their pieces you can tell them, pointing out the importance of seeing what the other player does.

Problem:
My child keeps losing and is getting frustrated.

Solution:
Children make more progress when they both win and lose at games. If they are assisted to "win" too often, they get a false sense of the actual challenges involved in the game. If they lose quickly, badly, and often, they could get frustrated or decide not to play the game.

It is highly recommended to balance winning and losing when teaching them.

Problem:
My child gets upset at the other player when he loses.

Solution:
Take the opportunity to teach your child to be a good sport. Chess players ought to have very good manners.

Teach them to shake the other player's hand and say "Good game," whether they win or lose. Get in the habit of doing this with them after each game.

You also want to make sure that you never get upset if they beat you. Your child is watching you like a hawk and will copy your behavior and attitude.

Problem:
My child thinks that this is boring and wants to move on.

Solution:
If they have shown you that they can attack pieces, defend them, and move out of danger, they can move on. Don't keep them playing this mini-game if they have these elements down.

However, if they can't show you these points, there could be a few things going on.

If you're letting them win too much and they aren't really figuring things out for themselves, they can get bored. Deep down they know they aren't really winning.

It is good to show them correct moves now and then, but let them try out their own ideas and make moves for themselves too. Encourage them to try things out. Allow them to make mistakes and to learn from them.

If they're having trouble moving the pieces, and now you're trying to introduce strategy, they could "get bored." It just means you went too fast through the other chapters and need to do a little review. Make sure they can move the pieces correctly most of the time before playing this mini-game.

Problem:
My child still moves the pieces wrong from time to time.

Solution:
This is normal and is to be expected. One of the reasons why you should stick with this mini-game for a while is that these two pieces are commonly confused. As long as they get the movements right most of the time, the practice will reinforce the correct movements.

If they are making a lot of errors, it is a good idea to do a quick review of the piece movements. Just take one of the pieces and review it and then take the other and go over the movements again. You don't need to do all the steps, just revisit the highlights.

Problem:
My child doesn't want to go on to the next chapter. She really likes this mini-game!

Solution:
Let them play this mini-game for a while. They will learn a lot from it. If you want them to move on, tell them that in the next section they will learn about the most powerful piece on the board, the queen. Chances are they'll be interested.

The Queen

9

fter the rook and the bishop, the next piece to learn about is the queen.

Step 1: Here's how the queen moves

Start by setting up the board with the queen in the center of the board:

Diagram 9.1

1a. Tell your child how it moves: Tell your child that the queen can move forwards, backwards, sideways, and diagonally.

1b. I point to the squares: Point to all the squares where the queen can go.
Since the queen moves like both a bishop and a rook, it's a good piece to learn now.

While you point out all the squares, tell your child that the queen is the most powerful piece on the board.

Diagram 9.2

1c. I move the queen: Move the queen around the board, making sure to move it in all directions. For instance, you might move the queen up three squares, then diagonally two, down one, sideways four, diagonally across the board, etc.

Of course, you should remember to take your hand off the piece after each move.

After you have moved the queen a few times, quickly point out all the squares it can go from its new position.

Step 2: Mini-game: I move, you move

Set up a single queen in the center of the board. Alternate moves with your child using this one queen, back and forth, back and forth.

This mini-game might be easy for your child, since they have had thorough practice with the bishop and rook. They'll be familiar with the queen's basic movements. Nevertheless, some children will only move the queen either up and down (like a rook), or they will just move it diagonally (like a bishop), forgetting the queen's full range of mobility.

Make a move with the queen and invite them to move. At the start of this mini-game, just look for correct moves.

Make sure to move at a pace they can handle. Match the speed they set.

If they only move the queen like a rook, remind them that the queen can also move diagonally. Encourage them to make some diagonal moves.

Likewise, if they only move the queen on diagonals, remind them that they can move it forwards and backwards as well as side to side.

When you see that they are varying their movements (also the shorter and longer distances across the board), start speeding up your moves. See how fast you both can move the queen around the board.

Step 3: The queen can't just go anywhere

Sometimes it can seem to children that the queen can just go anywhere. It is very powerful, but it has definite limits.

Start by showing your child correct moves and then make an incorrect one and say, "The queen cannot go here."

Here is an example of an incorrect move:

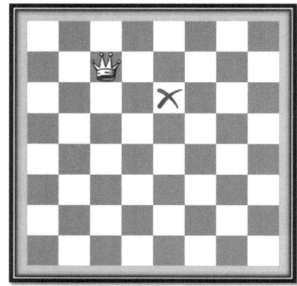

Diagram 9.3

Tell your child that the queen must still follow a line. In diagram 9.3 it isn't.

Give other examples that show the queen moving all the way across the board, but which are incorrect, like this:

Show them a lot of correct moves and a few incorrect moves.

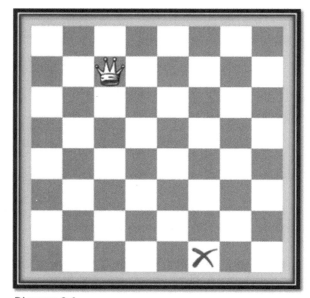

Diagram 9.4

Step 4: Mini-game: Can the queen go here?

In this mini-game, you will test your child's ability to correctly point out moves the queen can and cannot make. Start slowly by making a few moves that are correct.

Move the queen forwards, then side to side and then backwards. Then throw in a diagonal move and see if they think this is a correct move. Then throw in an incorrect move, one that you discussed in the previous step.

Keep asking your child about moves, increasing your speed slowly and matching their ability to keep up while still answering your questions correctly.

Step 5: The queen is very valuable

Although it may be obvious to your child, it is worth mentioning that the queen is worth more than the bishop or the rook. In fact, it is worth more than both pieces combined, but just by a little.

The message you want to give your child is that a trade of a queen for a rook or bishop would not be good.

Step 6: Mini-game: You get four pieces, I get a queen

Set up this position:

Tell your child that you will play the queen and they will get two bishops and two rooks. Explain that their four pieces together are better than the queen.

Diagram 9.5

Let your child know that they should try to hold on to as many pieces as they can. If they get down to only one piece, it isn't much of a game, so you should start over.

White goes first. Move your queen forward until it is attacking one of the rooks, like so:

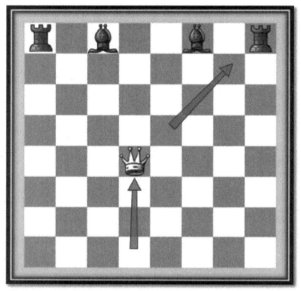

Diagram 9.6

If your child misses that their rook is attacked (which is very common when this game is first played), ask, "Am I attacking anything?"

If they have trouble seeing that your queen is attacking their rook, ask them to point out all the squares where the queen can go (you can help them with this). This is a good exercise to do periodically, as it gets them looking at the full range of a piece.

Now they need to figure out how to save the rook. Make sure they move it to a square where it is safe.

Then attack another piece and see if they spot it on their own. Again, help them find the attack.

After a while, you can start taking their pieces, making a game out of it.

Show them that the queen can attack two pieces at once. For instance, say the queen attacks the rook as above and the rook moves like so:

Diagram 9.7

Now you can move your queen here:

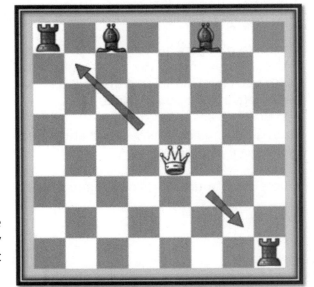

Give them a moment to look at the position and then ask, "How many pieces is my queen attacking?" Get them to show you both rooks.

Diagram 9.8

Now ask them to solve the problem, so that they don't lose either rook. One correct solution is to protect one rook with the other, with one solution being:

Diagram 9.9

This is just one example, but you will see other ways to attack two pieces at the same time with the queen.

Your child will learn that if they can guard their pieces the queen should not take them. In the above example, if the queen took the rook, it would be taken back. That would be a bad trade (and in this case the mini-game would end because White would have no pieces left on the board to move).

Through this mini-game, they will also figure out how the queen attacks and will be more aware of its power.

Keep playing until your child has figured out how to hold onto their pieces, by guarding them.

Step 7: Mini-game: I move, you move with rooks, bishops, and queens

Set up this position:

Diagram 9.10

Normally the queens would sit on the board across from each other, but with this mini-game we put the black queen in a different spot so that it couldn't get taken on the first move. We also did this with the rooks.

The focus here is to practice all the skills that your child has learned, together in one mini-game. At first the focus will be on moving all the pieces correctly. That's an important step.

When you see they have the movements down, start attacking their pieces, encouraging them to get out of danger. Also, put your pieces in danger now and then and see if they notice that they can take.

When your child can move these three pieces with ease, attack your pieces, take pieces, and protect their pieces, you can move on.

This is a mini-game that you can play over and over. It is a good idea to go back to it, even when you've read further ahead in the book. It is an excellent review of a number of key concepts.

Troubleshooting Tips

Problem:
My child has trouble moving the queen.

Solution:
If they have the bishop and rook movements down, but are having trouble mastering the queen, work with them a bit more on the mini-game, "I move, you move."

Work with your child to point out all the squares where the queen can go. You point out some and have them point out some.

Another variation of this is to put pieces on the board on all the squares where the queen can go. It would look something like this diagram, which shows all the squares that the black queen in the center can go to:

Diagram 9.11

Problem:
My child still thinks the queen can go anywhere on the board.

Solution:
It is important to actually tell your child that the queen cannot just go anywhere. It is a common misconception that children have, as the queen can move to many different squares. They start to think of the piece as an all-powerful superhero!

Make a point of spending some time on Steps 3 and 4. Show them many examples of incorrect queen moves, as well as correct queen moves.

Problem:
In the mini-games, my child keeps putting his pieces in danger.

Solution:
If your child moves their pieces into the path of your piece, ask them, "Can I take that piece?" If they continue to move into danger, have them point to all the squares each piece can move to on the board.

If they still have trouble, go back to the mini-game, "Attacking and Protecting." Spend more time with this one.

Problem:
My child doesn't notice when I've attacked her piece.

Solution:
If your child misses an attack, give them another chance to get out of danger. Try to re-create that kind of attack again later in the game and see if they spot it.

There is probably a pattern you can observe. Are they missing the long diagonal attacks? If so, have them point to all the squares where the bishop can go (or the queen). If they are missing rook movements, have them point out all the squares where the rook can go.

If they have trouble with the bishops and rooks, go back to the mini-game with just those two pieces. It's important not to rush past that too quickly.

When you play that mini-game, pick a piece and ask your child to point to all the squares where one piece can go. Then play a few more moves and ask about another piece. If they miss squares, help them point out all of them.

After they are confident about that mini-game, go back to this one, with the queens on the board.

Problem:
My child doesn't notice when he can take my piece.

Solution:
When you move a piece of yours into attack, and your child doesn't notice, allow them to take back the move. Ask them, "Can you take any of my pieces?" If they can't spot the piece, point to one piece at a time and ask, "Can that piece take mine?"

If they answer "no" with certainty (and are correct), move on to the next piece. If they aren't sure, have them point to all the squares where the piece can go. This will give them confidence that the piece cannot take yours.

Eventually, they will find the correct piece. Once they do, allow them to take your piece. The victory will still be sweet.

Problem:
My child is bored with this mini-game, but doesn't seem to get it.

Solution:
Go back to the bishop-and-rook mini-game and set up more positions where your child can take your pieces and you can threaten to take theirs. If they don't have that exercise down, they won't like the one with the queen. The queen is harder to understand and can be overwhelming if the rooks and bishops aren't understood.

The King

10

The king is an easy piece to learn, especially coming after the queen.

Step 1: Here's how the king moves

1a. Tell your child how it moves: The king can move one square in any direction.

Diagram 10.1

Also let them know that although the king cannot move very far, it is the most important piece on the board. Explain to your child that their job is to protect the king and attack the other player's king.

It might be tempting to get into an explanation of check or checkmate here (if you know these terms), but don't, as those are much more advanced concepts. We will touch on them in the upcoming chapters.

1b. I point to the squares: Point to all the squares where the king can move.

1c. I move the king: Move the king one square at a time, making sure to let go of the piece after each move. Move it forward, diagonally, sideways, and backward. This should be a quick demonstration.

Step 2: Mini-game: I move, you move

Make a move with the king and then have your child make a move. Alternate moves as you would with the other mini-games. Be sure that your child shows you that the king can also move diagonally, as well as forward, backward and side to side.

Step 3: The king can move like this, it can't move like that

Since the king is limited in movement, it is important to reinforce the idea that it can only move one square at a time.

Make several moves that are correct king moves and then jump the king two squares and tell your child that the king cannot move like that.

Make additional correct moves and incorrect moves. This should be a quick drill.

Step 4: Mini-game: Can the king move like this?

Make a few correct moves and then move the king two squares and ask, "Can the king move like this?" Continue to ask about correct moves and incorrect ones. Speed up the game until they have it down cold.

Step 5: The king can take, too

Set up this position:

Diagram 10.2

Since the king has such limited movement, beginners can forget that it, too, can take pieces.

Show your child that the king can take a piece too. Here the king can take the bishop.

Set up other examples for your child. You can use the rook, bishop or queen, but not the other king. We'll go over why in more detail later.

Check

11

his is an excellent point to introduce the idea of "check."

Step 1: This is what "check" means

1a: Give your child a simple definition: Explain to your child that check simply means that the king is being attacked.

1b: Here are examples of check: Show them an example of check. Set up the board like this:

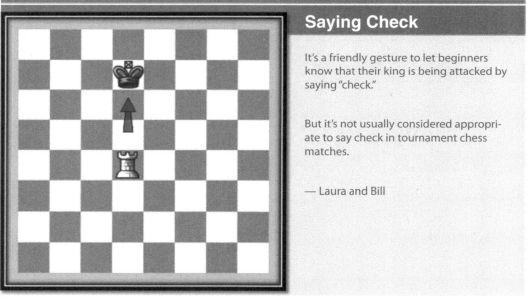

Saying Check

It's a friendly gesture to let beginners know that their king is being attacked by saying "check."

But it's not usually considered appropriate to say check in tournament chess matches.

— Laura and Bill

Diagram 11.1

Explain to your child that the black king is in check by the white rook. The rook is attacking the king.

You can also tell your child that some people say "check" when they put the king in check. It's a good habit for your child to get into at this stage of their chess development.

By the way, some people who don't fully understand the rules say you must say check when attacking the king. That isn't true. It is not a rule in formal competitive chess.

Now set up this position:

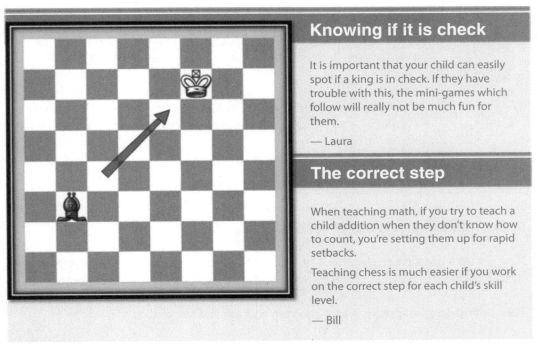

Knowing if it is check

It is important that your child can easily spot if a king is in check. If they have trouble with this, the mini-games which follow will really not be much fun for them.

— Laura

The correct step

When teaching math, if you try to teach a child addition when they don't know how to count, you're setting them up for rapid setbacks.

Teaching chess is much easier if you work on the correct step for each child's skill level.

— Bill

Diagram 11.2

Here the black bishop is checking the white king.

These are both check. Show your child many examples. Use the queen to check the king, too.

Step 2: You put the king in check

Place the king anywhere on the chessboard and hand your child the rook. Ask them to place the rook so that the king is in check.

If your child hesitates, ask them to tell you what "check" means. If they are unsure, tell them, "Check means that the king is being attacked." Then show them more examples. Trace a line from the piece, which is doing the checking, to the king.

If they get it right, have them show you another way to check the king with the rook.

Next, give them a bishop and have them do the same thing. And finally, give them a queen and have them show you check.

Coffee Talk

The victory of "check!"

Children will often feel that they've had a victory if they can put you in check. I've seen kids jump up and give an enthusiastic "CHECK!" when they attack my king.

You'd think they'd won a game!

Step 3: Mini-game: Is this check?

Now set up a position that is check (just use two pieces for this exercise). Ask your child, "Is this check?"

Then set up another position and another, and ask the same question.

After a few positions that are check, set up one that isn't and ask, "Is this check?"

Keep setting up different positions, using only the king and one other piece. Make sure that some are check and some not. If you see that they are getting the answers correct, speed up the process, until you are confident they have it.

Step 4: I move the king out of check

Explain to your child that when the king is in check the next move must cause the king to no longer be attacked.

Tell your child that you never take the king off the board. This is an important point to stress. Explain that you'll never see the kings taken off the board. Ever! If the king is attacked, something must be done to get it out of direct attack.

One way to do this is to move the king so that it is no longer in check.

Set up this position:

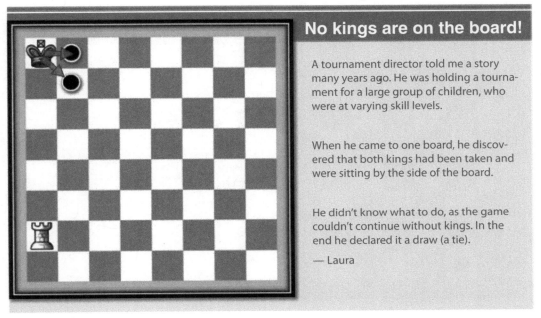

Diagram 11.3

Point to the two squares where the king could move, so it is no longer in "check." You can also move the king to these squares to show your child.

Point to the square right in front of the king (the one which does not have a dot). Show your child that the rook attacks that square. If the king moves to the square attacked by the rook, it would still be in check. Moving the king to an attacked square is not allowed.

The king can never move into check. It cannot put itself in danger.

Now set up this position:

This drill is important

This exercise is crucial for your child. Later they will learn how to win a game of chess. This skill will help them with that a lot!

— Laura

Teach them not to move into check

It is good for your child to have this skill down cold. It is important to start seeing quickly where the king can and can't go.

— Bill

Diagram 11.4

Point to the two squares where the king can move, telling your child that these are the squares where the king would not be in check.

Point out the square on the diagonal, which would still put the king in check. Let them know that the king couldn't move there.

You can also set up a position with the queen and the king, with the king in the corner and the queen checking the king along the diagonal. The more examples you show them, the better.

Then show them examples where the king is on the edge of the board, in check by a piece. Point to the squares where the king can and cannot go.

Step 5: Mini-game: You move the king out of check

Now set up a position with the king in the corner. Put the king in check, using either a bishop, queen, or rook. Ask your child to move the king out of check.

If they have trouble with this, ask them to tell you what check means. Make sure they understand the word. If needed play the mini-game, "Is this check?" a little more. Then ask again for them to move the king out of check.

Make sure they show you all the squares where the king can go.

If they had any difficulty with that position, set up a similar position in another corner and ask them to move the king out of check.

Use all four corners if you need to. The point is to continue to quiz them until they can move the king out of danger.

Now place the king somewhere on the edge of the board, putting it in check, like so:

Diagram 11.5

Ask your child to point to all the squares where the king can go.

This is a little trickier, because there are more places where the king can move safely. In the beginning it is fine to help them come up with the squares.

Set up a few positions where the king is on the edge of the board, before moving on to putting the king in the middle, like so:

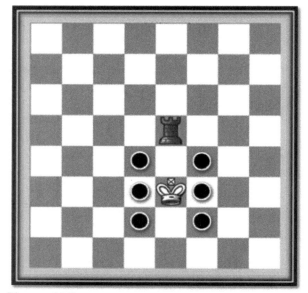

Diagram 11.6

This is harder, because there are more places for the king to go. When your child can figure out all the squares where the king can go, move on to the next mini-game.

Step 6: Mini-game: Can the king go here?

Now set up a position like this:

Start by asking your child, "Is the king in check?" making sure that your child knows this isn't check.

Now move the king to different places and ask, "Can the king go here?" (Note: there are three squares where the king cannot go because he'd be moving into check.)

Once they have gotten this, set up a new position and ask the same question. Once they get the hang of the exercise, speed it up. Ask them rapidly, "Can the king go here? How about here? And here? Here?"

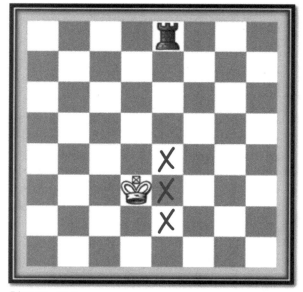

Diagram 11.7

The purpose of this mini-game is to get them to see when their king would be moving into check, so that they can avoid that.

Step 7: Kings can't go next to each other

Now that they have the concept that they can never move their king into check, you need to go over the fact that their king can never move next to the other king.

Set up this position:

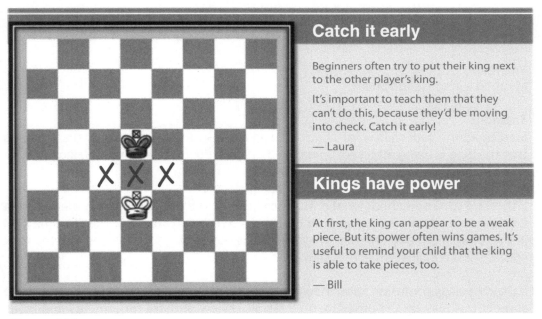

Catch it early

Beginners often try to put their king next to the other player's king.

It's important to teach them that they can't do this, because they'd be moving into check. Catch it early!

— Laura

Kings have power

At first, the king can appear to be a weak piece. But its power often wins games. It's useful to remind your child that the king is able to take pieces, too.

— Bill

Diagram 11.8

Discuss with your child what would happen if one of the kings moved forward. If they don't see a problem with this move, start by asking, "Can a king take a piece?" If this point isn't clear to your child, review Step 5 in Chapter 10, "The king can take, too." It's an important concept.

Once that's understood ask, "Can a king move into check?" Discuss this point with them. Now go over why a king would be moving into check if it moved next to another king.

Step 8: Mini-game: Can the king move here?

Now quiz your child on this one point, "king vs. king." Just set up a position like the one above, move one king, and ask, "Can the king go here?" Move it to squares that are next to the king and to squares that aren't. Make sure your child has this concept down. This should be a fast mini-game.

Troubleshooting Tips

Problem:
My child cannot set up check.

Solution:
Start by asking your child what "check" means. Make sure they understand that it means that the king is being attacked. Some children will add in other things, making it more complicated.

If they are confused about what check means, remind them (by showing them) how a bishop could attack a rook. Point out how the rook is being attacked. Then put the king in the rook's place and tell them that the king is now being attacked, just like the rook was. It just has a different name, "check."

If they have any confusion about how the pieces move, these exercises will not fly. If you suspect this may be the problem, do a simple review of these movements and make sure that your child knows how the pieces move.

Problem:
My child cannot figure out where the king can go to get out of check.

Solution:
Make sure your child understands check. Then play a quick round of the mini-game, "Is this check?" Make sure they have this down.

Next, show them many examples of how the king can get out of check. Have your child help you work out the solutions.

When you begin the mini-game "You move the king out of check," make sure to start with the king in the corner. It's much easier than starting with the king in the center or the edge of the board. Then use all four corners if they have any trouble.

Although the answers from the four corners are very similar to one another, they are slightly different and will help your child practice this mini-game.

Problem:
We're on the mini-game, "Can the king go here?" and my child is bored.

Solution:
If they're getting the answers correct, speed up the mini-game. Make it super fast and it will capture their interest.

If they are getting the answers wrong, it means that they don't understand something about check or need more work with the earlier mini-games. If they can use a piece to put the king in check, work with them to figure out squares where the king can and cannot go.

Make sure that you don't let them sit too long and "think" about where the king can go. If they're doing that, it probably means that they don't understand something about the mini-game. Help them with the "Can the king go here?" mini-game and then go back to the previous mini-game. Make sure that they can do those mini-games correctly and rapidly.

If your child cannot correctly spot the squares where the king can go, chess will not be a fun game. This is an important step for them to master!

Checkmate

12

T he concept of checkmate is much more advanced than check. This chapter keeps it very simple.

The purpose of this chapter

It is important to know some fundamentals about checkmate, because that is how one wins a game of chess.

At this stage, all you want to do is give your child a basic understanding of checkmate.

We will cover checkmate in more detail later in this book. There are a few other concepts that we need to cover before we can delve into this topic more fully.

It is worth noting that beginners often have a poor understanding of checkmate. This is because people often rush into this concept, before teaching some very important basic concepts that make checkmate much easier for new players to understand.

It's a little like teaching multiplication when addition isn't really fully understood. A child might be able to memorize a multiplication table, but they won't really get how to multiply. And they never will until they learn how to add.

In this book, we give you a solid foundation of building blocks which you can teach to your child. This will enable them to see how to checkmate other players and win games.

Step 1: This is checkmate

First, make sure that your child thoroughly understands check. If it has been a few days since your last lesson, take a few moments to review the idea of "check."

1a. Tell your child what checkmate is: Explain to your child that "checkmate" is when the king is in check and cannot get out of check.

Tell them that the way you win a game of chess is to checkmate the other player.

Remind your child that you never take the king off the board. Checkmate is the end of the game.

Coach's Corner

Someone told me ...

One four-year-old student came up to me one day, asking, "Another player said that you win at chess by taking the king off the board. I told him that wasn't right. Was I right?"

You should have seen the enormous grin that boy had when I told him that he was right!

— Laura

1b. This is not checkmate: Set up this position:

Diagram 12.1

Review with your child where the king can and cannot go. Here the king can move out of check, so this is not checkmate.

1c. This is checkmate: Add a rook as shown here:

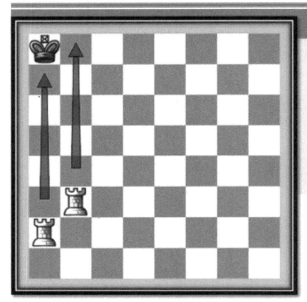

Diagram 12.2

Mate

Chess players often refer to checkmate as "mate."

Both mate and checkmate are acceptable and will be understood by skilled players.

— Laura and Bill

This is checkmate.

It's checkmate because the extra rook is now attacking those two squares.

Step 2: Now you show me checkmate

Set up this position:

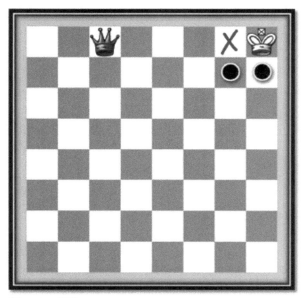

Diagram 12.3

X's and O's
The white king can only go to the squares with the black dots. It cannot go to the square with the X.

Have your child point to all the squares where the king can and cannot go.

Now ask your child to place a black rook on the board so it is checkmate. It needs to cover the two squares that have circles on them.

Although this position is very similar to the previous one, it is different enough that it will probably be a puzzle for your child.

Here are two possible solutions:

Diagram 12.4

Diagram 12.5

If your child has any difficulty with this, help them find a correct solution. Then put the king in a different corner, place the queen on the board so the king is in check, and have your child place the rook so it is checkmate.

Use all four corners if needed. It's valuable to make up examples in different corners more than once.

Step 3: These positions aren't checkmate

Now show your child various positions which look similar but aren't actually checkmate. Discuss with them why these positions are not checkmate.

Here are some examples:

Here the black king can move out of check. Make sure your child sees this.

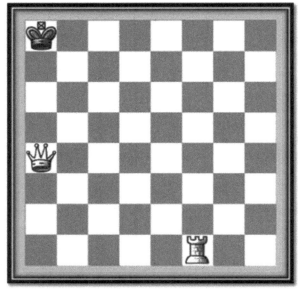

Diagram 12.6

Be sure your child sees that White can take the rook. This solution is often missed by beginners.

Diagram 12.7

The important thing to go over here is that the black king is not in check. The king must be in check in order for it to be checkmate!

Diagram 12.8

Step 4: Mini-game: Is this checkmate?

Set up similar positions to those in Steps 2 and 3 and ask, "Is this checkmate?" Start with positions that are checkmate and then set up positions that aren't.

Keep the king in the corner and only use the rooks and queen to checkmate it.

Troubleshooting Tips

Problem:
My child cannot figure out how to create checkmate.

Solution:
The first step is to review check. Start by asking your child what "check" means. Then ask them to give you an example of check.

Next review with them the various mini-games in Chapter 11. If they don't understand any part of this, checkmate will be impossible.

Also make sure that you have the king in the corner and that you've shown them many examples.

Problem:
In the mini-game, "Is this Checkmate?" my child can't tell me which position is checkmate and which isn't.

Solution:
If your child understands "check" and can do all the mini-games from the previous chapter, but cannot spot checkmates, show them more examples. Show them examples of positions that are checkmates and of ones that aren't.

See if you can spot a pattern of difficulty. For instance, if they have trouble spotting that the king can take a piece to get out of checkmate, you might want to review the chapter on the king. Show them more examples of how a king can take another piece.

The Knight

13

he knight can be one of the most challenging pieces to master. Part of the reason for this is that it is often taught incorrectly from the start.

It is likely that your child is very eager to learn about this piece. It is often a favorite piece of students.

A little discussion about the knight

The knight is the least understood piece. Even tournament players can miss potential moves by this piece.

Its movements are quirky and odd. They take some getting used to.

It all comes down to how you teach this piece's movement right from the start.

A knight moves like this:

Diagram 13.1

Alternate names

It's best to stick with the proper name for this piece, "the knight." Children will often call this piece a "horse" or "horsey." One two-year-old called it "nighttime" when she first learned the names.

— Laura

Thinking ahead

When your child goes to a tournament or club, it is best that they call this piece a knight, as that is what the other players will be calling it.

— Bill

So how do you teach this piece?

Step 1: The horse and fence

Diagram 13.2

Knights ride horses

Children often ask me why this piece is shaped like a horse. I ask them what a knight rides and they smile.

— Laura

It's a good idea to reinforce that knights are the only piece that can jump over other pieces.

— Bill

135

Note: If you have played a game or two, you know that the pawns never go on the first or last row of a chessboard. In this position, don't think of these as pawns, but as pickets of a fence!

Explain that the knight is like a horse and a horse can jump over a fence. It is the only piece that can jump over other pieces. Other pieces cannot jump over their own pieces or the other player's pieces. The knight always hops over the fence to a square just on the other side, which is a different color than the color it started on.

Now that's a mouthful. So you'll want to say it, but then break it up into bite-sized parts.

Step 1a: What to say: Here's how the conversation usually goes:

Set up the board as shown in diagram 13.2. Ask your child, "What color square is the knight on now?"

"Light."

"Good. Now, it needs to jump over the fence…where's the fence again?" Have the child point to the black pawns on the board.

"Right! Now, the knight needs to jump over the fence, to a color different from the color it started on. It's on a light square so it needs to hop to a…?" Pause, letting your child know you'd like them to answer.

"Dark square."

"Yes! So there are two squares it can hop to now. Can you find one of them?"

Note: You don't need to follow this exact conversation. It is just an example.

Step 1b: What to have them do: You want them to practice this simple direct hop (which some chess teachers call an "L"), right from the start.

When you ask them to find a square for the knight to hop to, they are likely to point to a square. Let them know they are correct and then have them move the knight there.

Now have them hop the knight back to the corner.

Get them to make as many hops as they can!

Now you can ask your child, "Can you find the other place the knight can go?" Have them hop the piece there.

If there was any hesitancy from your child, set up the same position in another corner, one with a different-color square, and quiz them on the two places the knight can go. Make sure they hop the knight to both.

Step 1c: What mistakes they might make: When a child is learning about the knight, there are two common errors:

- They move the knight too far. The solution is to just remind them that the knight can only go to the other side of the fence (the fence is squares next to the knight).

- They move the knight to a square that is of the same color as the square where the knight started. Just remind them that they need to hop the knight to a square that is of a different color.

Step 2: Now let's make the fence bigger

Now set up the following position:

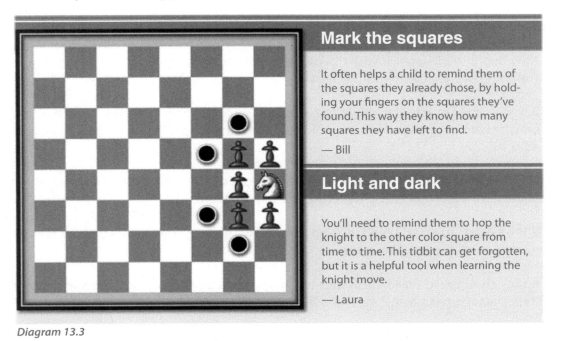

Mark the squares

It often helps a child to remind them of the squares they already chose, by holding your fingers on the squares they've found. This way they know how many squares they have left to find.

— Bill

Light and dark

You'll need to remind them to hop the knight to the other color square from time to time. This tidbit can get forgotten, but it is a helpful tool when learning the knight move.

— Laura

Diagram 13.3

Ask your child to tell you what color square the knight is on (it is on a dark square now).

Ask them what color it needs to hop to (it will need to hop to a light square).

Ask your child to find one square the knight can jump to. Have them hop the knight there and hop it back.

There are four possible squares where the knight can jump in this position. Have your child try to find all four, making sure they hop it back to the initial square each time.

It doesn't matter in what order they find the four squares.

Your child may not find all four. In this case, you can give hints.

If your child hops it to a square they have hopped it to before, tell them that they are correct and ask them to find a new square.

If they easily and very quickly find each of the four possible squares, move onto the next step. If they had any trouble, move slowly, or need hints to find the correct answers, set up the same position on the other side of the board, making sure to have the knight start on a light square now.

Step 3: Now just hop the knight

Now that they are familiar with this movement, start the knight in the same position as the last exercise, but remove the "fence."

Ask your child to hop the knight to one of the squares where it can go. Since they are familiar with this position, they should easily hop the knight to one of the four correct squares.

Now ask your child to hop the knight again (from that new location). They may think about it for a few moments. This is normal and expected.

If they make an error, simply remind them how the knight moves and show them a square where the knight can hop.

If they continue to make errors, put the knight back on the side of the board, place a "fence made up of pawns" around it and have them practice it a little more.

Have them continue to hop the knight around the board, encouraging them to move faster and faster.

This exercise is one that they should practice now and then. It really helps to learn and understand the unique movement of the piece.

Step 4: An additional exercise

Place the black knight in the center of the board and ask your child to point to all the squares where the knight can go.

Place a white pawn on each of the squares they indicate.

The resulting position will look like this:

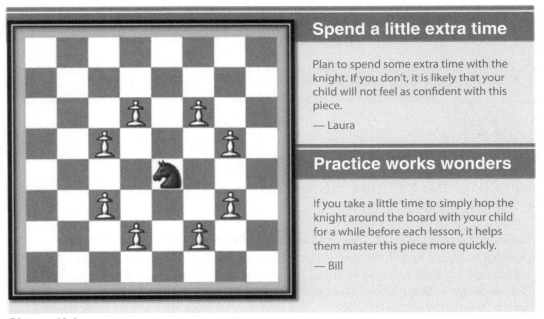

Spend a little extra time

Plan to spend some extra time with the knight. If you don't, it is likely that your child will not feel as confident with this piece.

— Laura

Practice works wonders

If you take a little time to simply hop the knight around the board with your child for a while before each lesson, it helps them master this piece more quickly.

— Bill

Diagram 13.4

Now have them practice taking each of the pawns with their knight, one by one. They should hop their knight back to the starting position each time, before taking the next pawn.

Step 5: Mini-game: Can the knight take this piece?

Set up the board with the knight and a piece that the knight could take. Ask your child, "Can the knight take this piece?"

Move the attacked piece to a new square and ask, "Can the knight take the piece now?"

Set up different positions, some where the knight can take the piece and others where it cannot.

Step 6: Mini-game: Knight – Is this check?

Set up a position where the knight is checking the king. Ask your child, "Is this check?"

Set up different positions with just the king and the knight, some which are check and some which are not. Ask your child, "Is this check?"

Troubleshooting Tips

Problem:
My child has Step 1 (knight in the corner) down, but cannot do Step 2 (knight on the side of the board).

Solution:
Go back to Step 1 and make sure they can spot the two squares where the knight can go very quickly. If they can't point them out immediately, they need a little more practice. Use all corners. When they can hop the knight to both squares within a few seconds, your child should try Step 2 again.

When they first do Step 2, it is fine to help them locate all four squares. Then set up the position on another square along the edge. The pattern will start to look familiar.

Problem:
My child can do the exercises with the fence, but cannot hop the knight around the board.

Solution:

The first step is to make sure that they can spot all four squares from the side of the board with confidence. If they can hop the knight back and forth to the four squares within 10 seconds or so, then they have it.

If they still have trouble making the hop, tell them to imagine the fence around the knight. You can even place a fence around the knight in the middle of the board to give them the idea.

You can also point to a square where the knight can go. Then point to another and guide them across the board.

Allow them to take their time in the beginning to find the correct square. Once they get the movement, they will speed up.

The Pawn

14

The pawn's movements are surprisingly complicated, because there are so many parts to explain.

Many people make the mistake of starting with the pawn when teaching, because it is the weakest piece on the board.

This sets up the first lesson for failure, as it can be too much for a beginner.

Looking back over all the pieces, you'll probably better understand why it is best to teach the pieces in this order. The rook is a great place to start, because the movements are straight. It's pretty easy to grasp immediately.

The bishop introduces the concept of diagonal movement, which might take some practice. The nice thing about the bishop is that it just has one type of movement (diagonal).

Then the queen uses both straight and diagonal movements, which your child now understands, so it is a logical piece to teach next.

The king is easier to explain, but there are nuances that are complex (check, checkmate, and the fact that a king can't move next to the other king). So it's best to go over the king after learning about the queen, rather than before.

The knight has a complex movement, so it comes next. It is still easier than the pawn, because it only has one set of rules about how it moves.

So now that your child has mastered the rook, the bishop, the queen, the king, and the knight, it is time to teach them about the pawn.

Step 1: Here's how you move the pawn at the start of the game

The diagrams are set up so that White is at the bottom of the board and Black is at the top.

Explain to your child that the white pawns start on the second row and the black pawns start on the seventh row. From the pawn's starting place, it can move either one or two squares forward, like so:

Diagram 14.1

Diagram 14.2

Make sure they understand that this choice is only available for each pawn's first move. Each pawn has this option for its first move.

Step 1a: You move the pawn to start: Put a white pawn on the second row and have your child make the first move. They are simply moving the pawn one or two squares forward.

After they make this move, move the pawn to a different spot on the second row and have them make its first move again.

Next place a black pawn on the seventh row and have them make a starting move for Black (again moving it forward one or two squares).

Step 2: This is how the pawn moves after the first move

Show your child that after the first move the pawn can only move one square forward as its basic movement.

It can never move sideways or backwards. A pawn only ever moves forwards.

Have them practice this, by moving the pawn down the board, one square at a time, until they only have one square left. Have them stop at this point.

Step 3: Something cool happens now

Tell your child that when the pawn reaches the other side, something really cool happens. You can make a big deal about this.

This is one of the most popular moves in chess with kids. The little pawn is replaced by another piece!

3a. Defining "Promotion": Tell your child that the word "promotion," in chess, means that when a pawn reaches the last row it can turn into a queen, rook, bishop, or knight. (It cannot turn into a king or stay a pawn.)

You may never have two kings of the same color on a chessboard.

You may, however, have two queens (or more) of one color.

Some sets come with an extra queen for both sides. That is because if a player gets to the last row and promotes a pawn, they will usually choose to promote it to a queen. If they already have a queen in play, they will need another.

There is a common misconception that you may only promote a pawn into a piece that was taken off the board. This isn't true. The rule is that you may promote a pawn into any piece, except for the king.

3b: I promote the pawn: March the pawn down the board, and when it reaches the last row turn it into a queen. This is done by taking the pawn off the board and replacing it with the other piece.

Then send another pawn down the board and turn it into a rook. Turn another one into a bishop and another into a knight.

Coffee Talk

That's not a pawn

One two-year-old girl was learning about the pieces. She would identify the bishop, knight, queen, king, and rook as "not a pawn."

She was making a point about how much she really liked the pawns!

Step 4: You move the pawn

Have your child start with a pawn on the second row. Have them move the pawn down the board. Make sure they take their hand off the pawn with each move. When they hit the last square, ask them to promote their pawn into any piece they like.

Most of the time your child would want another queen, but there are times when a different piece might be better.

Have them play with this as much as they like.

Step 5: The pawn takes differently than it moves

Show your child that when a pawn takes, it takes on a diagonal. It attacks and takes one square forward, diagonally. It never takes backwards. And it never takes pieces directly in front of it.

This is a bit tricky, because it is the only piece that moves differently than it takes. This is why the pawn is sometimes difficult for a child to master.

Here are two examples of how the pawn takes:

The white pawn can take the black bishop.

Diagram 14.3   Diagram 14.4

In diagram 14.5 the black pawn can take the white rook, because it moves in the opposite direction from the white pawns.

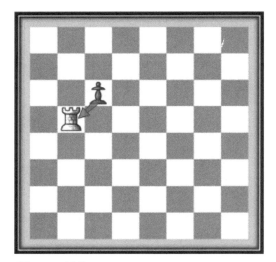

Diagram 14.5

Diagram 14.6

Show your child many examples of how a pawn can take other pieces (knights, rooks, bishops, queens, or other pawns).

After a few examples, have your child take a piece with the pawn, giving them practice.

Step 6: Pawns get stopped

Because a pawn takes differently than it moves, an odd situation comes up. Set up this position (one black pawn and one white pawn):

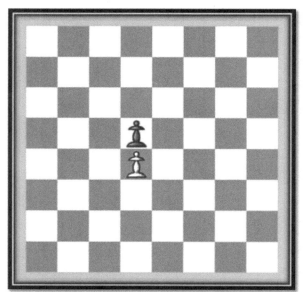

Diagram 14.7

Explain to your child that when the pawns are facing each other like this, the white pawn cannot move. It can't move forward, because the black pawn is in its way. It also cannot take the black pawn, because it doesn't take that way. It is stopped.

Point out that the black pawn is also stopped for the same reason.

Coffee Talk

Sumo wrestlers

One parent described blocked pawns as being like sumo wrestlers. They sit facing each other, unable to pass the other.

Her five-year-old daughter thought the image of two hulking men, sitting in the middle of the chessboard, was hilarious!

It's important to spend some time on this concept. Most beginners will find this strange and will want to take the pawn ahead of them.

Pieces can block a pawn as well, if they are in front of a pawn. Show this example:

Diagram 14.8

Now set up the following position (two black pawns and one white pawn):

Diagram 14.9

Show your child that the white pawn can now move, because it can take the black pawn one square diagonally. This is the only move that pawn can make.

Have your child take the black pawn. Now you will have this position:

Point out to your child that the white pawn can now move forward.

The black pawn can move too, since the white pawn is no longer blocking it.

Diagram 14.10

Set up more positions like this, giving them lots of examples of how the pawn can be stopped from moving forward, but can take.

Make sure to use pieces as well as pawns in your examples. Diagrams 14.11 and 14.13 are two examples:

Diagram 14.11

Diagram 14.12

Here it is White's turn to move. Ask your child if the white pawn can do anything.

Diagram 14.13

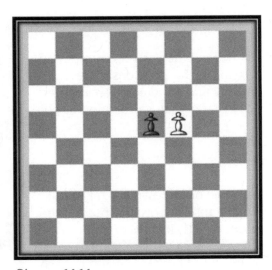

Diagram 14.14

Here it is Black's turn. Ask your child what the black pawn can do here.

Step 7: Mini-game: Can the pawn take this piece?

Now quiz your child on when a pawn can take and when it cannot.

Start by setting up simple positions where a pawn can take a piece of the opposite color. Ask your child, "Can the pawn take this piece?"

Then add in a few that are clearly not correct. Start with obvious incorrect setups, like this:

Diagram 14.15

Also set up positions where a piece is directly in front of the pawn.

As they get the answers correct, you can make the positions more complex by adding in additional pieces. For instance, you can set up this position:

Here the black pawn can take either White's pawn or bishop (but not the pawn directly in front of it).

If your child hesitates, point to each piece and ask, "Can the black pawn take this piece?"

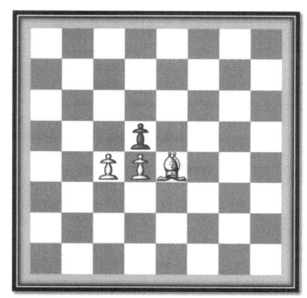

Diagram 14.16

Keep quizzing your child, increasing the speed as they answer the questions correctly (or slowing down if they start making mistakes), until they really understand how the pawn takes.

Step 8: Mini-game: Can the pawn move like this?

Now you want to quiz them on correct and incorrect pawn moves, putting together moving forward and taking diagonally. Start by asking a few obvious moves that are correct, like moving the pawn one square forward on an empty board, asking, "Can the pawn move like this?"

Have a pawn take a piece one square diagonally and ask, "Can the pawn move like this?"

Then throw in an incorrect move (like moving the pawn backward one square) and ask, "Can the pawn move like this?"

Make a few correct moves and then move the pawn incorrectly (perhaps sideways) and ask the same question.

Balance the correct moves and incorrect moves. Make sure to include these incorrect moves:

- Moving the pawn backwards.
- Moving the pawn forward more than one square (except from its starting square).
- Moving the pawn sideways.
- Taking a pawn directly in front of it.
- Taking a piece two squares away.
- Moving one square diagonally, when there is nothing there to take.

These are common errors that beginners will make when they are learning about the pawn. As they get the answers correct, speed up the game. When they can answer the questions quickly, you can move on to the next mini-game.

Step 9: Mini-game: What are all the ways the pawn can move?

In this quiz, you want to set up different positions and quiz your child on all the ways that the pawn can move.

For instance, you can set up this position:

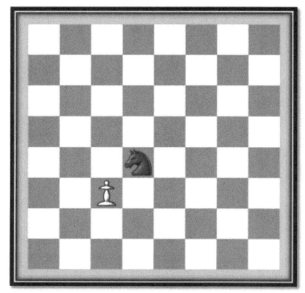

Ask your child to tell you all the ways the white pawn can move. They are likely to see that they can take the knight, but might miss that they can also move the pawn straight ahead.

Diagram 14.17

Set up lots of positions like this and quiz your child. Make sure some positions are ones where the pawn is blocked from moving forward. Here is an example:

Here the white pawn cannot move forward, as it is blocked by the rook. However, make sure your child sees that the pawn is able to take the knight.

Diagram 14.18

Here is another position you can quiz them on:

Diagram 14.19

When you give this position, remind your child that the pawn is standing on its starting square.

There is no value in trying to "trick" your child, but it is important to make sure they remember that they can move the pawn one or two squares at the start.

As they begin to get more and more answers correct, speed up the game, until they really have this down.

Step 10: Mini-game: Pawns vs. pawns

The following three mini-games have been popular teaching tools for decades among chess coaches. We didn't create these mini-games, but wanted to share them with you, as they are fun and instructional.

Put the pawns out on the board on their starting squares like so:

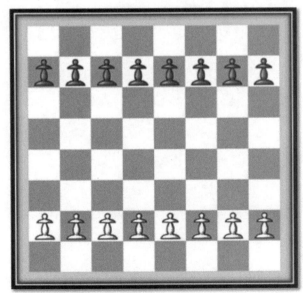

Diagram 14.20

The idea is to practice moving the pawns forward, as well as taking the other player's pawns on the diagonal.

When you do this exercise, make sure to capture some of your child's pawns and help them to take yours. Keep it as even as you can. You can give your child hints along the way.

Allow at least one of their pawns to get to the end of the board, so that they can practice promoting it into a piece. Continue the game, using the new piece as well as the pawns. You can stop playing at any time, restarting the game, if it becomes unbalanced.

There is no set place to end this game. If you wind up way ahead, feel free to start over. The only real purpose is to practice all the aspects of the pawn.

Step 11: Mini-game: Five pawns vs. a rook

Set up this position:

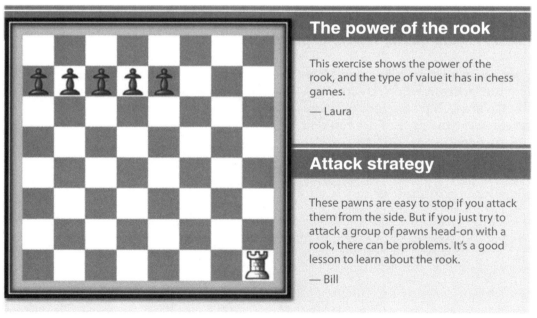

The power of the rook

This exercise shows the power of the rook, and the type of value it has in chess games.

— Laura

Attack strategy

These pawns are easy to stop if you attack them from the side. But if you just try to attack a group of pawns head-on with a rook, there can be problems. It's a good lesson to learn about the rook.

— Bill

Diagram 14.21

The side with the rook goes first. Your child should play this mini-game from both sides.

Step 12: Mini-game: Nine pawns vs. a queen

Set up the position below:

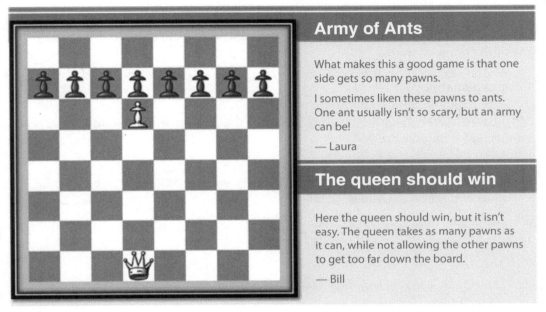

Army of Ants

What makes this a good game is that one side gets so many pawns.

I sometimes liken these pawns to ants. One ant usually isn't so scary, but an army can be!

— Laura

The queen should win

Here the queen should win, but it isn't easy. The queen takes as many pawns as it can, while not allowing the other pawns to get too far down the board.

— Bill

Diagram 14.22

Note: Since your set only has 8 pawns, you will need to "borrow" a white one for this exercise to make a ninth black pawn.

Ask your child if they would rather have 9 pawns or a queen. Allow them to take the side they prefer.

The queen gets to go first.

If the side with the pawns is able to promote a pawn into a queen and hold onto it for at least a turn (that is, not immediately lose it), that side wins. Otherwise, if the queen can take all the pawns, that side wins.

This is a powerful little exercise. There is quite a bit of strategy that your child can learn here.

Make sure to switch sides and allow your child to play the side with the queen as well as the side with the pawns.

Step 13: Optional: An odd little rule

This is another rule about pawns that comes up, but not too often. It is included here so you have all the rules regarding the pawn's movement.

Unless your child will be playing with strong players in a chess club, you shouldn't go over this step with them.

Basic explanation

"*En passant*" is French for "in passing." It is a rule that is often misunderstood (and is very confusing for beginners).

Coach's Corner

What kids say

En passant is a tricky concept for children. Our students will often ask to go over "that weird French thing" with them a few times.

It's a concept that takes a while for most children to get.

Here's how it works. Say you have this position:

Note: White has a pawn on their fifth row. Black has a pawn one file (column) over on their starting row.

Diagram 14.23

If Black were to move their pawn up two squares, like so:

Diagram 14.24

White could actually take it! It would look like this:

Diagram 14.25

Here White took Black's pawn *en passant*.

You only have one chance

In the above example, White can only take the black pawn right after Black moved it two squares forward. That's White's only chance.

In a game situation, if White makes a different move, the option to take this particular pawn *en passant* would be lost.

The logic

It's a bizarre-looking move, but when you think about it, it's quite logical.

The first thing to remember is that a pawn always takes one square forward, on the diagonal. That rule still applies to this situation.

Also, you can consider that the black pawn was taken "in passing." It started on its second row and landed on the fourth, but was taken as it was passing through the third row.

Why this rule exists

The rules of chess have evolved over time. There was a time when pawns could only move one square at a time.

When the rule changed to allow a player to choose between moving the pawn one or two squares on the first move, there was one problem.

In this setup, the fifth-row pawn would never get a chance to take the second-row one.

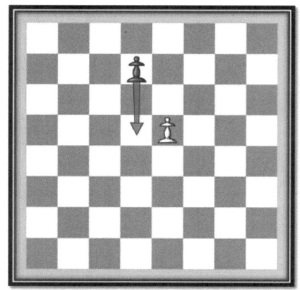

Diagram 14.26

To avoid this situation, *en passant* was developed, giving the player one chance (and only one chance) to take the pawn.

Troubleshooting Tips

Problem:
My child continues to try to take pieces in front of the pawn.

Solution:
This is a common error and one that is solved by practice. Remind your child that a pawn takes differently than it moves. Then show them many examples of how it can take and how it moves. Make sure to show them how a pawn gets stopped, too.

Set up positions like this:

Diagram 14.27

Quiz your child on what the pawn can do in diagram 14.27.

Here's another:

Diagram 14.28

Ask your child what choices the white pawn has.

Give them lots of positions like this and make sure they see that they can't take the pawn directly in front of them.

Problem:
My child moves the pawn backwards and sideways.

Solution:
Remind your child that a pawn can never go backwards or sideways, that it only moves forwards.

If you feel this might be a point they will forget, make a little mini-game of asking them things like, "Can a pawn move sideways? How about forwards one square? How about backwards?"

Then you can have them "quiz" you, using the same questions.

Next, show your child how a pawn moves and then give them examples of how the pawn cannot move. Give them lots of examples of correct moves and incorrect moves.

Now go back to the Step 8 mini-game, "Can the pawn move like this?" Then quiz them more on this section.

Problem:
My child wants to move the pawn more than one square at a time.

Solution:
Remind them that they can only move the pawn two squares on the pawn's first move. It only has that choice once.

Have your child move the pawn down the board, one square at a time. Make sure they are using proper form each time (taking their hand off the pawn with each move).

Next, quiz them on correct and incorrect pawn moves with this one concept in mind. Move the pawn one square forward, asking, "Can the pawn move like this?" Then move the pawn three squares, and ask again.

Problem:
My child has trouble seeing all the different ways a pawn can move.

Solution:
Start with simple positions where the pawn only has one choice. Give many examples of these, working with your child to find the move, until they can confidently do it on their own.

Then set up positions where the pawn has two choices. Work with your child again to help them solve the puzzle until they can do it on their own.

If you see that they have trouble spotting a particular move pattern, work on that with examples, showing that movement.

Then you can start showing them puzzles with more possibilities.

Problem:
My child is frustrated with the "Nine pawns vs. the queen" mini-game.

Solution:
Although this is a mini-game, it is also an exercise. It is important that your child experience winning this mini-game. Work with your child, allowing them to take back moves, so that they can win.

Give them pointers. Help them to understand that the pawns are more valuable when they are protecting one another. Show your child that if they send a pawn all the way down the board by itself, it won't survive.

When they play the side with the queen, help them realize that they need to pay attention to the pawns, making sure they don't get too far. However, in order to win this, they need to take a pawn with almost every turn.

Legal and Illegal
CHESS MOVES

15

I t is important for your child to learn which moves are legal in chess and which are not. If they start playing in tournaments, they will need to know this and be confident in spotting move choices that are legal.

Kids enjoy using these two phrases, legal move and illegal move. They tend to grasp the concept quickly.

Step 1: Let's go over what legal and illegal moves are

1a. Tell your child what it means: Explain that in chess, there are certain moves which are "legal" and some that are "illegal." Tell them that "legal" means that they are allowed to make the move. "Illegal" means that they cannot, because it is against the rules.

Be sure to explain that this is different from "illegal" where the police will come and arrest people. You don't get in trouble with the law for making an illegal move. You just aren't allowed to do it.

1b. Show them examples: Show them examples of illegal moves with each piece. For instance, moving the bishop forward three squares like a rook is an illegal move.

It is a good idea to show that taking your own piece is illegal.

Moving past a piece that is blocking a long-range piece, like a bishop, rook or queen, is also not allowed.

And make sure to show them how moving the king into check is an illegal move. Include a position where one king moves next to the other and remind them that this is illegal. It helps to repeat this concept a few times.

If you make an illegal move, you must take the move back. If that happens, you must then make a correct move.

Step 2: Mini-game: Is this legal?

Set up a position with a few pieces on the board. Quiz them on different moves, asking them if the moves are legal or illegal. Start with simple legal moves (like a rook move or a bishop move). Then throw in some illegal piece moves.

Then you can ask about which king moves are legal and illegal. When you start this mini-game, give them plenty of time to answer. As you progress and see that they can answer, encourage them to answer quickly. Make it an exercise of speed, where they must answer as fast as they can.

When they can answer quickly and easily with a variety of positions, it is a good time to continue to the next section.

Step 3: Show me legal and illegal moves

Put the queen in the middle of the board.

Have your child show you a legal queen move and an illegal queen move.

Do the same with each piece.

Also make sure they show you illegal king moves. Set up this position:

Diagram 15.1

Ask them to show you legal and illegal moves with the king.

Troubleshooting Tips

Problem:
My child cannot grasp the difference between legal and illegal.

Solution:
Be sure that they understand the terms, "legal" and "illegal" and aren't just nodding their heads while you explain. Have them tell you what these terms mean, using their words.

If they still have trouble, give them lots of examples. Each time go over with your child what it is about the move that makes it legal or illegal. Start with something simple, like moving the rook diagonally. Ask, "Can the rook move like this?" Since they did this mini-game in the rook chapter, they'll probably remember that it cannot move that way. Now point out that this would be an "illegal" move.

If they have trouble with king moves, review the chapter on check. Make sure they know where a king can and cannot move.

Problem:
My child is bored and doesn't want to do the exercise anymore.

Solution:
If your child is getting all the answers right, they know it and you can move on.

If they aren't getting it, but they don't want to do it anymore, get them to tell you what legal and illegal means. Make sure it is correct. If they are having trouble with a certain kind of move, review that area. For instance, if they are having trouble knowing where to move the king, review the chapter on check, which goes over this.

Also let them know that this is important for the game. They can't play if they don't know the rules.

Their boredom most likely comes from the fact that you're moving either too fast or too slow for them.

How to Set Up
THE CHESSBOARD

16

fter learning how the pieces move, it's time to learn how to set up the board.

Step 1: This is how you set up a chessboard

Explain to your child that the pieces always start in the same place when you play a game of chess.

Start with all the pieces off to the sides of the board.

Make sure that the lower right corner is light. Light goes on the right. Show your child that this is a light square. If they know their right from their left, you can tell them that the right square is light.

The expression commonly used is "White on the right," but this can be confusing if the light square isn't white.

If they don't know which side is right, just point out that "this" square (pointing to the child's right) should be light.

1a. This is where the rooks go: Explain that the rooks always start in the corners of the board and place them like so:

Diagram 16.1

Ask your child to place their rooks on the board, across from yours. When they are done, it should look like this:

Diagram 16.2

1b. This is where the knights and bishops go: Now that you have the rooks on the board, reach for the knights and explain that the knights go next to the rooks, and place them on the board. Have your child place their knights next to their rooks.

Next put the bishops down, explaining that they go next to the knights. After your child places their bishops on the board, it should look like this:

Diagram 16.3

1c: This is where the king and queen go: Now you can tell your child that the king and queen go in the middle, in-between their two bishops.

Pick up your queen and explain that it always goes on its own color. The white queen will sit on the light square, and the black queen will sit on the dark square. Ask your child, "Since my queen is white, which square should I put it on?"

After they point to the correct square, place the queen there and explain that the king goes next to it.

Now ask them to point to the square where their black queen should go. If necessary, remind them that the queen sits on its own color. Ask your child to place the black king next to the queen.

The board should now look like this:

Diagram 16.4

1d: This is where the pawns go: Now place all eight pawns on the board in front of the pieces.

Invite your child to do the same with their pawns. In the end your board should look like this:

Diagram 16.5

Step 2: Now you set up the board

Put all the pieces to the side of the board again and ask your child set up the board on their own. Help them as needed. The common errors are:

- Switching the squares for the knights and bishops.
- Placing the queen on the wrong square.
- Orienting the board incorrectly, so that the lower right corner is dark.

Allow them to practice setting up a board a few times. It isn't vital that they get this down perfectly now, as they will practice this every time they set up a board.

Coffee Talk

"The pieces were all wrong!"

There is a certain power in knowing the correct way to set up a board. Children are often pleased when they can spot boards set up incorrectly in stores and in photos.

One six-year-old boy said he corrected the store owner one day. "The pieces were all wrong!" he said.

Step 3: Mini-game: What's wrong here?

Now set up the board so that there are errors. Have your child tell you what's wrong with the setup.

Here are two diagrammed examples of how you might set it up incorrectly:

Knights and bishops

It is common for children to mix up the starting position of the knights and bishops.

If they start a game with the pieces in the wrong place, they will get used to the wrong starting position. Later they will develop incorrect strategies as a result.

— Laura and Bill

Diagram 16.6

Kings and queens

The rule of thumb that helps with the queen position is that the queen always sits on its own color.

If the king and queen get mixed up, it will throw the game off dramatically.

— Laura and Bill

Diagram 16.7

For a third incorrect starting position, rotate the board 90 degrees and have them notice that the square on the bottom right is dark (not light).

Troubleshooting Tips

Problem:
My child doesn't know left from right.

Solution:
This isn't a problem. You can find ways around that. It really only comes up when you orient the chessboard. Your child can remember that the light square goes on "that" side. Show your child both the correct way to position the board and the incorrect. They will see where the light square goes.

Problem:
My child switches bishops and knights around.

Solution:
Talk to your child about the pieces. Help them come up with a way to remember it. Quiz them by asking things like, "So, does the knight start out next to the rook?" or "Does the bishop go next to the king and queen at the beginning of the game?"

You can also have them quiz you. Make a game out of it!

Problem:
My child forgets to put the queen on its own color.

Solution:
If your child forgets this rule, simply remind them. Quiz them with questions like, "Does the queen go on its own color?" or "If the white queen were placed on the board, would it go on the light square or the dark?"

These little quizzes can be asked at any time. If you're preparing dinner with them, driving in the car, etc. just ask them these little quiz questions. They will get it!

Problem:
My child doesn't notice when the board and pieces are not set up properly.

Solution:
This takes practice. If they make errors, go back to Step 3 and make a game of having them fix the errors.

You can also practice setting up the board a few times with them. First you do it, explaining what you are doing, and then have them set the board up.

The First Game

17

ow you and your child are ready to start your first full game of chess!

As you play your first games, take it easy.

All you are trying to accomplish with your first game is to make sure they are moving the pieces correctly, while giving them the thrill of playing a game from the starting position.

There is no need to play a complete game right away.

If you know how to play chess, you might be tempted to teach strategy.

Don't.

It is hard enough to remember how all the pieces move correctly. Let your child practice this for a while.

Expect your child to make mistakes. Simply remind them how that piece moves. If they consistently move a piece incorrectly, do a review of how that piece moves. To review, you might need to clear the pieces off the board to go over that piece's movements. To resume your game, set up the board again.

It's a good idea to practice taking pieces in this game. Try to keep things even, if possible. Don't just allow them to take all your pieces, while you avoid taking any of theirs. Trading pieces is an important part of chess.

What to watch out for

The only pieces you can move at the beginning of a game are the pawns and the knights. Make sure your child doesn't hop over the pawns with any of the other pieces.

Also make sure that your child doesn't take his own pieces or try to put two pieces on one square.

It is a lesson all on its own that your own pieces actually block your movement. Your pieces can get in your own way! We'll go over this more in another chapter.

Don't forget to notice if a king is attacked. Help your child to remember that this is check.

If you or your child checkmates the other player, the game is over. This probably will not happen in this game, but watch out for it in case it does.

Enjoy your first game with your child! If you don't finish a complete game, that's fine. Often it's better not to even attempt it.

The purpose of the first game is just to move the pieces properly. The first game requires no strategy at all.

Troubleshooting Tips

Problem:
I don't know how many moves to make in the first game.

Solution:
Remember that the first game is just about learning to move the pieces. We'll get into a bit of strategy in the next chapter. For now, you just want to see that they can take pieces and comfortably move the pieces around the board.

It's always good to keep the lessons short when your child is young. Play the first game for fifteen minutes or so and then offer to end the game. Congratulate them for playing their first game of chess.

If they are super-excited and want to play more, let them. Just be sure to stop while it is still fun.

Problem:
My child is making bad moves.

Solution:

Don't correct anything but incorrect piece movements. In the next chapter, we'll go over some strategy on how to start a game. It is okay for now that they make any move, as long as it's a legal move.

It's one thing to learn how to move each piece, independently, and another to learn how to move them all on the board when they are together. When they can move each piece correctly and you're satisfied that they have this down, move on to the next chapter.

Problem:

My child is making a lot of errors in piece movement.

Solution:

It is natural that they will make mistakes, because now they are putting together all the pieces' movements.

When they make an illegal move, help them.

If you notice a pattern of error, go back to the mini-games of the chapter which covers this.

For instance, if they are having trouble hopping the knight, practice with just a knight on the board. Set up the pawns around the knight (as in the mini-game in Knight Step 4: An additional exercise) and ask them to take each pawn with the knight.

As you play with your child, your child will learn each piece's movement better and better and will make fewer and fewer errors.

Problem:

My child is only moving the pawns.

Solution:

Encourage them to use all their pieces. Chances are that they are moving their pawns because they are shy about trying out the other pieces.

You can suggest moves for them, to get them started.

It's important in these early games that they show you how each piece moves.

Make sure that when it is your turn, you move pieces as well as pawns.

Problem:
We just played a long game and my child wants to play again.

Solution:
Your child will sometimes push to continue to play if you let them. It's best to end the lesson and promise to play again tomorrow.

Usually, if you give in, they will play for a while and then get less interested. It's worse to end at this point.

Castling

18

ow that your child has had a chance to play their first game, it is time to teach them a very important move – castling.

This move is more complicated than the others, so it is important to break it down and practice it a bit first.

Step 1: Here's how you castle

Explain to your child that castling is the only move in chess where you can move two of your own pieces on the same turn. It is a special move with special rules.

Show your child how to castle, while explaining how it is done. Start with this setup:

Diagram 18.1

Pick up the white king and move it two squares toward the rook. While you do this, tell your child, "This is the only time in chess when you can move the king two squares!"

Next, let go of the king, pick up the rook, and move it to the other side of the king.

Diagram 18.2

Tell your child, "This is castling!"

Note: You should only use one hand for this move. First you move the king two squares and then you put the rook on the other side. Avoid using two hands.

Do this a few times. It looks strange at first, but soon your child will get it.

Step 2: Mini-game: Did I castle right?

It's a good idea to show your child incorrect ways to castle, so that they can see the mistakes one can make with this complex move.

Start by castling correctly and ask, "Did I castle right?" Now reset the king and rook, and then have the two pieces switch places (a common mistake). Ask, "Did I castle right?"

Make other incorrect castling moves and then castle correctly. Make sure your child really understands when you are castling properly and when you aren't.

Step 3: You castle

Now have your child do it. Remind them to move the king two squares and put the rook on the other side.

Encourage them to use one hand. When a child uses two hands to castle, they often get confused and put the pieces on the wrong squares.

Have them do this step until they no longer hesitate.

Step 4: You castle for Black

Set up the black king and rook in their starting positions and have your child castle for Black. Although it is the same move, the position is different and they may need to practice this a few times.

If you feel your child needs to see it first, show them that the king moves two squares and then the rook goes on the other side.

Diagram 18.3   Diagram 18.4

Step 5: Castling often looks like this

Diagram 18.5   Diagram 18.6

Show your child how to castle in this position. You might say something like, "I'm going to castle the same way I did before. First I move the king two squares and then I put the rook on the other side."

Step 6: You castle in this position

Now have your child castle using the position given in diagram 18.5.

Set up a similar position for Black and let them practice castling for the other side as well.

Step 7: Here are all the rules of castling

When you see that they are consistently moving the pieces correctly, tell them that there is a little more to learn about castling.

Rule 1: In order to castle, you must not have any pieces between the king and the rook. Set up this position:

Diagram 18.7

Explain to your child that in this setup (diagram 18.7), White cannot castle because the knight is in the way.

Rule 2: You cannot castle if you have moved the king earlier in the game. Explain that even if the king moves back to this square, you may not castle, because the king moved.

Show an example of how the king could move twice, landing back on the square it started. Explain that they wouldn't be able to castle in this case.

Rule 3: You cannot castle with a rook that has moved earlier in the game. Again, show how this would be, by moving the rook back and forth, putting it back where it started.

Note: There are other rules of castling that are more complex. We've included them in Step 14, but suggest that you not go over these until they've gained more experience with the game.

Step 8: Let me show you what you need to do to castle

Start with the white pieces all in their starting positions. Make three moves which would allow you to castle. Here is one possible end position:

Tell your child that you are all set to castle now.

Now reset the pieces and make three different moves to ready yourself to castle. Keep doing this until you feel they have it down.

Diagram 18.8

Step 9: You show me what you need to do to castle

Now set up the same position for your child. Have them make three moves to prepare to castle.

Once they have done this, tell them to castle.

Do this until they are confident in these moves.

Step 10: Let's play a game and castle!

Now set up the board in the starting position and play through a game. It isn't important to finish. You are simply letting them practice castling in the setting of a real game.

After you have played a few moves, tell them that you'd like to show them more about castling. Remember: do not get into any discussion about strategy. They are still practicing moving the pieces.

Step 11: The king can castle queenside, too

11a. Explaining kingside and queenside: Explain to your child that the chessboard is divided into two sides. Show your child that the kingside is the side where the king starts. If one is playing White, it is the right side of the board. If one is playing Black, it is the left side.

Use the words "right" and "left" only if your child is comfortable with these terms.

Diagram 18.9

And the queenside is the side where the queen starts.

Diagram 18.10

11b. *This is how you castle queenside:* Tell your child that they can castle kingside or queenside in chess.

Set up this position:

Diagram 18.11

Now pick up the king and move it two squares toward the rook. Let it go and pick up the rook and put it on the other side.

This is known as "castling queenside."

Diagram 18.12

Tell your child that the king always moves two squares when castling. Then the rook goes on the other side. It doesn't matter which side they are castling on, the same rule applies.

Have your child practice this a few times. Set up the king and the two rooks in their corners and have them show you how to castle kingside and queenside.

Now do the same on Black's side, using the black pieces, having your child practice castling there too. Again, you should encourage your child to use one hand.

Note: Some people have a misconception that the king moves three squares, instead of two, when castling queenside. This is incorrect.

Step 12: Here's why castling is a good idea

Discuss with your child about why castling is a good move. Ask them for their thoughts on it. Do they think the king is safer in the middle of the board or tucked away in the corner?

If they say the center, ask them to imagine they had a box of treasure that they had to protect. Would they rather be in the center of a large room where people could try to take the treasure from all sides? Or would it be better to be in a corner, where the walls offer protection?

Now ask your child about the rook. Do they think it is better out in the center or in the corner? Help them to see that the rook can do more after it has castled.

Step 13: Mini-game: Can I castle now?

Quiz your child on the points of castling.

Start with the starting position and make moves so that you wind up with a position where White can castle (like this one):

Diagram 18.13

Now ask, "Can I castle now?" If they have difficulty with this, quiz them on the three rules of castling.

Now move the white king up one square. Then move the black bishop out and move the white king back again. The position will look like this:

Diagram 18.14

Then ask "Can I castle now?" If they have trouble with this, review the three rules of castling again. The correct answer is that White cannot castle because the king moved.

Now ask, "Can Black castle?" Make sure they see the difference and that Black can castle.

Now set up this position:

Diagram 18.15

Let your child know that no one has moved their rooks or kings. Ask your child to show you all the ways that both sides can castle.

Next, tell them that White's queenside rook has moved. You can show this by moving it over one square and back. Tell your child that White's kingside rook has not moved. Ask, "Can White castle queenside?" and then ask, "How about kingside?"

Now set up this position:

Diagram 18.16

Ask, "Can White castle?" Find out which side. Then ask if Black can castle (and ask which side).

Keep quizzing your child, using positions similar to these, until they have this down.

Step 14: Optional: More on castling

This section should be skipped for now.

It is included here to give you a complete understanding of all the rules of castling.

Teach them these advanced rules when your child has gained experience and they're ready to play in a more advanced setting.

Along with the basic rules of castling, there are three times when one may not castle:

- You can't castle into check.
- You can't castle to get out of check.
- You can't castle through check.

14a: You can't castle into check: Here is what castling into check would look like:

Diagram 18.17

Diagram 18.18

This one is straightforward and obvious. Since you can never move your king into check, it makes sense that you cannot castle into check. It is still worth mentioning, as a beginner may not put this together.

14b: You can't castle to get out of check: Here's what castling to get out of check would look like:

Diagram 18.19

Diagram 18.20

This one isn't as obvious. In fact, it might seem like a logical escape. However, the rules of chess state that you can't get out of check by castling.

14c: You can't castle through check: Here is what castling through check would look like:

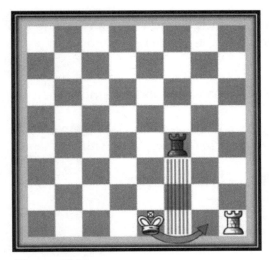

Diagram 18.21

Diagram 18.22

Here you see that in order for White to castle, the king must travel through a square that is covered by the black rook. This is not allowed.

Troubleshooting Tips

Problem:
My child is having trouble castling.

Solution:
Take all the pieces off the board and just focus on the king and rook. Help them castle and then reset the position and castle again.

It is important that they always follow the same pattern. Move the king two squares and then put the rook on the other side.

Problem:
My child castles with two hands.

Solution:
It is natural for a child to want to castle with two hands, because they are moving two pieces in one turn. However, if they use two hands, they often put one or both of the pieces in the wrong place.

The correct way to castle is to move the king two squares first and then move the rook.

If your child continues to use two hands, start by reminding them. Have them practice castling with one hand. And make sure that you yourself always castle with one hand.

You can also have them sit on one hand while they castle. This helps!

Problem:
My child doesn't understand the advanced rules of castling.

Solution:
Skip these rules until your child really understands all aspects of the game.

If you started teaching these rules and realized that your child doesn't understand them, simply end that part of the lesson and ask if they'd like to play another game.

Problem:
My child can't tell me when they can castle in "Step 12: Can I castle now?"

Solution:
Go over the rules of castling again. Show examples of each rule, so that they can see why they can't castle in that position.

Show them many more examples, illustrating positions where one side can castle and when they can't.

Have them show you examples where one side can't castle.

Then, show them a position where White cannot castle and tell them, "White can't castle. Can you tell me why?" Discuss it with them, helping them to understand.

When they have this down, repeat "Step 12: Can I castle now?" until they can spot when they can castle and when they can't.

Problem:
My child can castle kingside, but not queenside.

Solution:
Tell your child that when you castle you always move the king two squares and then put the rook on the other side. This rule is true for kingside and queenside.

Have your child tell you how to castle. If they are uncertain, tell them again (move the king two squares and put the rook on the other side).

Show them how to castle queenside a few times. Then have them make the move.

Next, have your child castle kingside and then reset the king and rook. Now have them castle queenside. Have them do this for White and Black.

Tips for How to Start
A GAME OF CHESS

19

N ow that your child knows how to set up a board and you have played your first games, you might wonder how to go about teaching your child some winning strategies.

An excellent point to begin learning sound strategies is the first few moves that occur at the start, or the "opening," of a game of chess.

Your child can become familiar with the simple (but master-level) principles that lead to a good position early in the game.

Step 1: Here is the center of a chessboard

You can explain about the center by placing an empty chessboard on the table. Point to the four squares in the middle, explaining that this is called "the center."

Explain that the center is important in a game of chess. If your pieces control the center, you will have an easier time controlling the game.

Diagram 19.1

Step 2: Let's go outside!

It is a good idea to give your child a clear sense for the importance of the center. Go to an enclosed field (perhaps at a school or a park). If you can't easily find this, you can also do this with a room (the larger the better).

Have your child stand in the corner or edge of the field (or room) and look around.

Then have them go out to the center and compare the feeling they have.

Go back to the corner or edge and ask them to pretend that they have to protect the whole field (or room) themselves. Do they feel that they can easily do that from the side?

Now bring them back to the center and ask, "Do you feel like you can be in control of this area better now?"

When you are in the center, you have more control. You can move in all directions more easily and are close to every point of the field from the center.

Explain to your child that the chessboard is like a field. You can control the space on the chessboard much easier if your pieces are in the center.

Step 3: Let's look at the knight

Now you can give your child another example, one that relates directly to chess.

Set up this position with a knight:

Ask your child to point to all the squares where the knight can go. In the diagram above, you'll see all the choices highlighted. You'll notice there are eight squares where the knight can go.

Diagram 19.2

Now put the knight at the edge of the board and have your child point to all the squares it can go:

Diagram 19.3

As you can see, the knight can only go to four squares.

Now set the knight up in the corner.

Diagram 19.4

Have your child point to the squares where the knight can move now.

Discuss with your child which spot is a better place for the knight to be, so that it can control the board. Help them to see that the knight in the center can do more and control more squares.

Note: This will also give your child a little refresher on the knight, which can be a tough piece to master. If they have trouble with the knight's movement, go back to the horse-and-fence exercise. It will come back to them.

If you feel your child could use more examples, you can place the bishop on the side of the board and then in the center, comparing the two.

Step 4: Where your knights and bishops should go

Set up the board (in the starting position) with your child. Tell them you will be going over the best moves to begin a game.

Tell them that it is best to move out the knights and bishops first.

4a. Moving the knight out: Show your child, on the board, the two choices here for the knight's first move:

Diagram 19.5   *Diagram 19.6*

Ask their opinion about which is the better move.

If they choose the one on the edge, remove the other pieces around the knight and have them point to the squares the knight covers. Then have them look at the other option and compare.

4b. Moving the bishop out: You may need to remind your child that in order to get a bishop out, you must move a pawn. Now show them where the bishop could go, if the pawn in front of the king were moved.

Avoid blocking pawns

The value here is that the bishop is out. However, the problem is that it is blocking the pawn in front of the queen. This might make getting their other bishop out harder.

It is a good idea to discourage this move, as it will make future moves more challenging.

— Bill

Diagram 19.7

Moving a piece in danger

Beginners sometimes miss that their piece can be taken, especially if it can be captured by a pawn.

This position is a common example. Help your child see that their bishop would be taken if they went here.

— Laura

Diagram 19.8

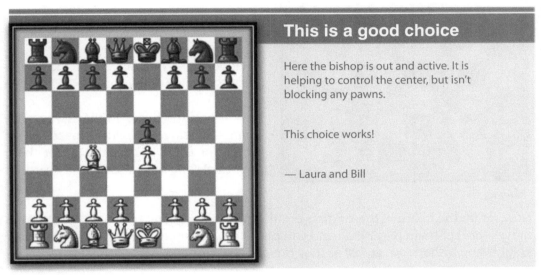

This is a good choice

Here the bishop is out and active. It is helping to control the center, but isn't blocking any pawns.

This choice works!

— Laura and Bill

Diagram 19.9

Diagrams 19.7 - 19.9 show three choices. Discuss with your child which is best and why the other two are not as good.

Step 5: Castle early

Remind your child that castling is a very good move. It is best to castle early in the game, so that your king is protected and your rook gets into play. Now that you have discussed the center with your child, the idea of getting the king out of the center is worth repeating.

Step 6: Mini-game: Move out the other knight and bishop

Set up the board in the starting position. Now have them work out how to move their knights and bishops out and castle, within seven moves. The end position might look something like this:

Diagram 19.10

Have your child show you all the center squares that they now control.

Next set up the board in the starting position and ask your child to make similar moves for Black. It is good to get them used to playing both sides of the board.

Now set up the board in the starting position and tell your child that you'll be making moves too. Let them play White and you play Black. Tell them to work on getting their knights and bishops out as fast as they can and also castle.

When your child gets all their pieces out, reset the board to the starting position and switch sides. Now you play White and let them play Black.

All you're doing here is helping them figure out how to get their pieces into play and take control of some center. If they want to continue the game you've started, that's fine. Just pick up where you left off next lesson.

Step 7: Here are places to put the rooks and queen

When you have a position where all the knights and bishops are out, tell them that it is time to move the queen and rooks out.

Explain to your child that by moving the queen one square forward, the rooks now protect each other and can move to more squares. The queen can also do more from this square.

Show your child that rooks are best placed behind the other pieces at the beginning of the game, offering support and protection.

Here are two examples of good setups for White's position:

Diagram 19.11

Knights and bishops first

It is usually best to move out your knights and bishops first, before bringing out your queen.

Although there are times when this rule isn't necessary, it is a great rule of thumb for a beginner.

— Laura and Bill

Diagram 19.12

Many excellent options

There are many choices. The only important thing here is to help your child make moves that control center squares.

— Laura and Bill

Step 8: Now let's play another game

Play a game with your child, keeping in mind that the pieces should be brought out toward the center.

You don't need to finish the game. All you really want to see is if they can move the pieces out, so that they are pointed toward the center.

Every now and then, ask your child to point to the center squares that their pieces control.

Make sure that your moves also control the center. They will be watching where you move your pieces very carefully!

Step 9: It's a good idea to get the pieces out quickly

Tell your child that it's a really good idea to get their pieces out quickly. In the previous exercises you've been doing this, but it is good to talk about this as a separate concept.

Discuss the idea that the pieces aren't doing much on the back row. Once you bring them out, each piece controls a lot more space.

When you bring your pieces out, it allows the king to castle to safety. Then the rooks can get out too.

Tell your child that there are some good things to know about how to start a game:

- During the first part of the game, don't move a piece twice unless you have a really good reason.
- Only move pawns out to get control of the center and to let the other pieces out.
- Castle as soon as you can.

These three rules will help your child get their pieces out quickly.

Note: If your child can take a piece for free, that would be an example of a really good reason to disregard one of the above points.

Discuss these three ideas with your child.

Give examples showing what problems you run into when you don't use these concepts.

It can be effective to be a bit over the top (or extreme) with the examples you give.

For instance, if White keeps moving their knight around the board while Black moves out all their pieces, after a while it's easy to see that wouldn't be good.

You can also have Black just move pawns, while White plays good moves. It might look something like this:

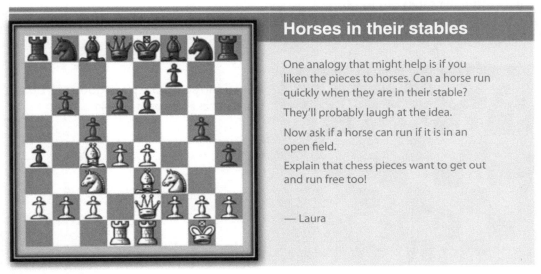

Horses in their stables

One analogy that might help is if you liken the pieces to horses. Can a horse run quickly when they are in their stable?

They'll probably laugh at the idea.

Now ask if a horse can run if it is in an open field.

Explain that chess pieces want to get out and run free too!

— Laura

Diagram 19.13

Ask your child which side they'd prefer to play. Have them look at the position from both sides and see what they can do.

Sometimes children think it is better to move pawns to start, but in this example it is clear that White has more options.

In this example you can also show that Black hasn't castled, so the king isn't safe.

Step 10: Let's play another game!

Now play another game, keeping the previous step in mind. Make sure your child follows the basic ideas listed above. Or, if they don't, then ask if they have a reason for breaking the rules.

Play a few games with these points in mind.

Step 11: Here are some things you don't want to do

There are some common errors a beginner might make. These are good to go over with your child.

Don't bring the rooks out too early

Show your child this position:

As you can see, this isn't as good plan. Black can just take the white rook!

Diagram 19.14

It is Black's turn. Ask your child, "What's a good move for Black here?" If they have trouble finding it, ask them to tell you all the squares Black's light-squared bishop can go.

Beginners often think that moving the rook out early is a good plan, because it activates a powerful piece. The problem is that this isn't a good spot for the rook. It can often be taken immediately (like in this position), but its movement also gets blocked by the other pieces as they come out.

It is best to move the rooks only after you castle. Teach your child that the rooks should come out later in the game. They tend to work better in the center of the back row.

Let your child know that if they play someone who moves a rook out early, they might be able to take it!

Don't bring the queen out too early

The queen is often a favorite piece with children, because it is so powerful.

Tell your child that if they bring the queen out too early, the other player will probably attack it. Then they'll need to move it again. Since it is so valuable, they will spend a lot of time moving away.

Ask your child to look at this position:

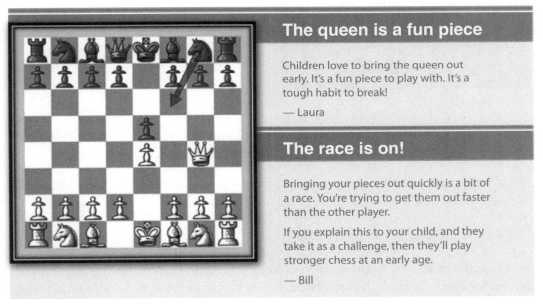

The queen is a fun piece

Children love to bring the queen out early. It's a fun piece to play with. It's a tough habit to break!

— Laura

The race is on!

Bringing your pieces out quickly is a bit of a race. You're trying to get them out faster than the other player.

If you explain this to your child, and they take it as a challenge, then they'll play stronger chess at an early age.

— Bill

Diagram 19.15

See if they can find a good move for Black now. Help them to see that if they bring out their knight they can chase the queen away and move a piece into play.

Now set up this position:

Diagram 19.16

Here the queen is sitting where the knight would usually go. Plus Black can find a way to attack the queen in a few moves, forcing it to move away.

Show your child more examples of how the queen gets chased around the board if it comes out too quickly.

Don't move the king so you can't castle

Remind your child that if you move your king, you cannot castle. Not castling makes it harder for you to protect the king because it is sitting in the middle rather than near a corner, where it is usually safest.

So it is best not to move your king until you castle.

Step 12: I make bad moves, you make good moves

Now explain that you're going to play a game with them, making moves that aren't good. Invite them to play well and see what happens. Talk to them about why your moves are bad and theirs are good.

Make all the mistakes we went over in the last step. Move your pawn in front of the rook and bring your rook out early, by moving it two squares. Encourage your child to take

the impulse to move just one piece will change when they do later exercises from this book.

Problem:
My child understands the pointers given about how to start a game, but doesn't use them in a game.

Solution:
Talk to them about their idea. If they have a good reason, it's okay.

Some children don't want to tell you, because they want to keep their plan a secret. That's fine, but after a few moves, you can look back over the game and discuss it with them. See if it worked out the way they thought it would. Chances are, it didn't. Talk about that and allow them to take back the moves.

It's good to let them try things out. They will learn a lot more that way than if they are forced to follow strict guidelines.

Value of
THE PIECES

20

In chess, you can get a huge advantage if you can get more pieces than the other player. It makes it easier to win.

Step 1: Mini-game: Who has more?

The first step is to help your child figure out who has more pieces.

If you start with positions which don't have a lot of pieces, it is much easier for a child to recognize who is winning.

Here is an example:

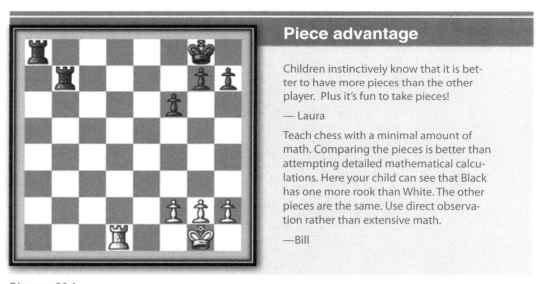

Piece advantage

Children instinctively know that it is better to have more pieces than the other player. Plus it's fun to take pieces!

— Laura

Teach chess with a minimal amount of math. Comparing the pieces is better than attempting detailed mathematical calculations. Here your child can see that Black has one more rook than White. The other pieces are the same. Use direct observation rather than extensive math.

—Bill

Diagram 20.1

Set up lots of positions like this. You can also set up positions with more pieces on the board, like this:

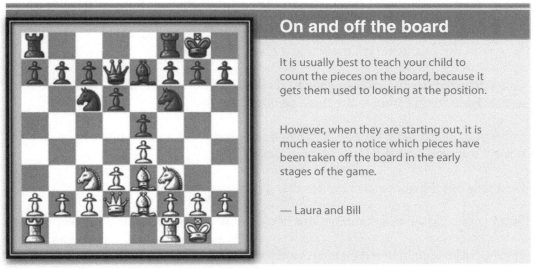

On and off the board

It is usually best to teach your child to count the pieces on the board, because it gets them used to looking at the position.

However, when they are starting out, it is much easier to notice which pieces have been taken off the board in the early stages of the game.

— Laura and Bill

Diagram 20.2

Here Black is missing a bishop.

In this mini-game, make sure one side always has an extra piece or pawn. Don't get into relative values at this time (like when one side has traded a rook for a bishop).

Step 2: This is how much each piece is worth

In order to know whether you should trade one piece for another, you must know how they compare.

For older children, you can use a point system, which many players use around the world. For younger children, math should be avoided entirely. Don't try to teach about addition. These lessons should just focus on chess.

2a. For older children who are comfortable with addition: Explain to your child that each piece has a certain value. In chess we say that they are worth a certain number of points.

Start with a pawn. Tell them that a pawn is worth one point.

Now take out a bishop and a knight. Explain that these are each worth three points.

Ask your child to show you how many pawns it would take to be worth a bishop. Make sure they actually bring out three pawns to illustrate the point.

Now take out a rook and tell them that it is worth five points.

Using different pawns, ask your child to show you how many pawns it takes to be worth a rook. Have them compare the three pawns to the five.

Show your child that if White had a black rook and Black had a white bishop and two pawns, this would be the same point value.

Next take out the queen and explain that it is worth nine points.

Show your child various combinations of pieces that would equal the value of a queen.

Finally, tell your child that the king is worth the game. It doesn't matter how many other points you have won. If you are checkmated, the game is over.

2b. For younger children: If your child isn't comfortable with math (addition and subtraction), don't talk to them about the point system. Instead, show them which pieces are worth more than other pieces. Give lots of examples.

For instance, ask them which they'd rather have, a pawn or a bishop.

Group some pieces together. Show them that a group of three pawns has about the same amount of power as one bishop.

Show them that trading a knight for a bishop, or a bishop for a knight, is usually pretty even.

Discuss this with them. Although a pawn can turn into a queen, a pawn isn't very powerful at the start of the game.

Show them how much better a bishop is than a pawn. It can do a lot more, cover more space, help other pieces, etc.

Also compare a knight to a pawn and discuss their values. Is a knight better than a pawn?

Note: Some people value the bishop a little higher than the knight, but this difference isn't important at this stage. It's much more important to keep things simple.

Now remind your child that a rook is worth more than a bishop or a knight. You went over that earlier in this book (in Step 8 of Chapter 8, "How to Attack and Defend Pieces"), but it is good to mention again.

Take out two white pawns, a white knight, and a black rook. Tell them that the value of the white pieces is about the same as the value of the black pieces in this case. Explain to them that the rook is about two pawns better than the bishop or knight.

Now take out a white bishop, a white knight, and a black rook. Tell them that the two white pieces combined are worth more than the black rook.

Your child already knows that a queen is worth more than a rook or a bishop. You can tell them that the queen is even a little better than both the bishop and the rook, combined.

If you give them lots of examples, over and over, they will learn about the values of the pieces without the use of math.

Step 3: Mini-game: Is this a good trade?

Quiz your child by showing them different combinations of pieces.

Start by asking about even trades. For example you could ask, "Is it okay to trade a white bishop for a black bishop?"

Then ask, "How about a white rook for a black knight?"

Quiz them on all the combinations you mentioned in Step 2.

Step 4: There are some times when points don't matter

It is a good idea to explain that there are times when points don't matter.

The point system is a good rule of thumb, but there are many exceptions to these rules.

Set up this position:

Diagram 20.3

Here White is about to promote a pawn. Black has a knight. Discuss with your child which side they'd rather play.

There are also other times when one piece will be worth more than it normally would be because of how it is positioned on the board. Recognizing these exceptions comes with experience. The exceptions aren't very important here, but should be mentioned briefly.

Troubleshooting Tips

Problem:
I taught my child the point system, but they are getting tripped up by the math.

Solution:
Do your best to take the point values out of the picture. Talk about relative values instead. Stress that a bishop is better than a pawn and a rook is better than a bishop or knight.

Once they are comfortable with addition, you can reintroduce the point system. It isn't really so important now, though. As they play, they'll increase their understanding of relative piece value in various positions.

Problem:
My child spends a lot of time counting the points of the pieces off the board.

Solution:
This is a hazard of teaching the point system to a young child. It is good to encourage them to focus on the pieces on the board, rather than the pieces off the board.

Problem:
My child has trouble with certain trades.

Solution:
Focus on the basic ones. Is a queen worth more than a rook? How does a pawn compare to a bishop?

It isn't terribly important at this point for them to know that two rooks are slightly better than a queen. This subtle difference doesn't affect their games at this level.

Your Pieces
CAN GET IN THE WAY

21

Step 1: Your own pieces can get in your way

Put a rook in the center of the board and point to all the squares where it can go.

Now set up this position:

Diagram 21.1

Show your child that the white rook's movement is now blocked by the white pawn. Point to all the squares where it can go. Now place another white piece on the board, so that it further blocks the rook.

It is important that your child understands that their own pieces can get in the way of the movement of their other pieces. The more blocked a piece is, the less valuable it is to you because it can't do as much.

Keep adding pieces until you get a position similar to this:

Diagram 21.2

Now point to the squares where the rook can move.

Do this exercise with the queen and bishop, as well. Start with the piece in the center of the board and then restrict the movement more and more, showing your child how that piece becomes blocked.

Also, remind your child how easily a pawn gets blocked.

Although the knight can hop over pieces, it too can be blocked in. Set up this position:

In diagram 21.3, the knight cannot move!

Diagram 21.3

Step 2: Mini-game: Point to the squares where the piece can go

Set up positions, similar to the ones in the previous step, for the other pieces, where one player's pieces get in the way of their own piece. Have your child point to the squares where that piece can go.

Set up positions where the piece can go to many squares, and others where it can only go to a few (or none at all).

Step 3: Mini-game: Point to the squares where the king can go

The king's movements can be blocked as well. This is an important concept to get across. When your king's movements are restricted, it's much easier to get checkmated.

Set up various positions where the king's movements are blocked by its own pieces. Have your child point to the squares where the king can go.

Here are some examples:

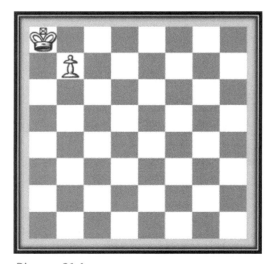

Diagram 21.4   *Diagram 21.5*

Diagram 21.6

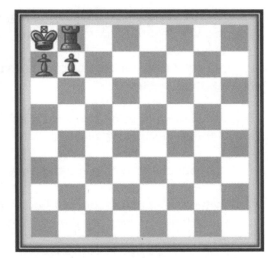

Diagram 21.7

Set up many examples and have your child point to the squares where the king can go (in diagram 21.7, the king is trapped by its own pieces).

All you want to do here is to get your child used to spotting the squares where the king can go. When they can do this accurately and very quickly, move on.

Step 4: What piece can move?

Set up the starting position.

The only pieces that can move at the start of the game are the knights and the pawns.

Help your child to see that the bishops, rooks, queen, and king are blocked in.

Diagram 21.8

It is good to go over how blocking relates to the start of the game. With this new information it will help to reinforce the importance of getting the pieces out quickly.

Ask your child if the white rook can move in diagram 21.8. Make sure they see that the rook has nowhere to go.

Now ask your child to find another piece that cannot move. And another. Have them find all the pieces that are blocked.

Next ask your child to show you the pieces that can move.

Work with your child to figure out how to get the light-squared bishop out. Have them spot the two pawns they could move to get that bishop out.

Let's look at moving the pawn in front of the king:

Diagram 21.9

Ask your child to point to all the squares where the bishop can now move. Get them to see how this piece can now become active.

Next, ask your child to find another piece that can now move. Get them to see that the queen now has places to go.

Although the king is able to move, remind your child that they will probably want to castle, so they shouldn't move the king.

Problem:

In the mini-game, "Point to the squares where the king can go," my child is missing some of the moves the king can make.

Solution:

Go back to a position where the king can only move to one square. Come up with several positions like that and then progress to a position where the king can move to two squares.

As you progress, you can start putting the king on the edge of the board or in the center. But understand that this mini-game gets harder when there are more places that the king can go.

Problem:

In the mini-game, "Point to the squares where the king can go," my child is picking moves that are two squares away.

Solution:

If your child points to a square next to the king and then to a square two squares away, it is likely that they are thinking two moves ahead. Remind your child that you are just looking for choices for the king for right now, not next move (even though visualizing a series of moves is wonderful).

If they are confused by how the king moves, thinking that it moves two squares at a time, simply review the king's movements with them.

More About
ATTACKING

22

hen someone learns to play chess, they sometimes overlook when their pieces are attacked. They can also miss opportunities to take the other player's pieces.

It is important to practice spotting both these points.

Step 1: Mini-game: Which of my pieces are you attacking?

Set up the board like this:

Diagram 22.1

Ask your child, "Which of my pieces is the black rook attacking?" If they have trouble with this, do a rapid review of Chapter 6, "How to Take the Other Player's Pieces."

You can also have them point to all the squares where the rook can move. This will uncover which piece the rook is attacking.

Give them a few more positions like this (with only three pieces) until they can confidently give you the correct answer.

Now place three white pieces and a black rook and ask them which pieces the rook can take. Vary the number of pieces the rook can take (one, two, or even all three).

Keep adding pieces, speeding up the game as you go. Here's an example of a harder position:

Diagram 22.2

Try different positions, using different attacking pieces. If your child has difficulty at any point, use fewer pieces. Remember, the more pieces that are on the board, the harder the exercise.

Step 2: Mini-game: Which piece is attacking which piece?

Start with positions where only one piece is attacking another. Here's an example:

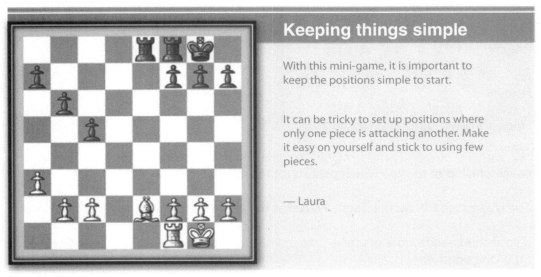

Diagram 22.3

Keeping things simple

With this mini-game, it is important to keep the positions simple to start.

It can be tricky to set up positions where only one piece is attacking another. Make it easy on yourself and stick to using few pieces.

— Laura

Ask your child if any piece, on either side, can take another piece.

Give your child a moment to look at the position. If they have difficulty, you can help them rule out a few pieces.

Start by pointing out that the kings can't take anything. Then show them that one of Black's rooks can't move. You can also have them look at all the pawns and see that none of them can take anything. Keep narrowing it down.

At first this may be tricky for your child. Set up more positions like this.

Long diagonals can be harder for children to spot, so wait a little before giving an example where a bishop is attacking a pawn from a distance.

When you feel that they are ready, here is an example you could use:

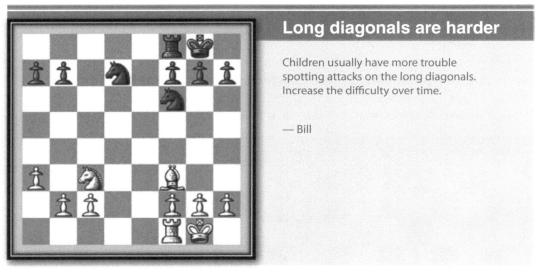

Long diagonals are harder

Children usually have more trouble spotting attacks on the long diagonals. Increase the difficulty over time.

— Bill

Diagram 22.4

Ask your child to tell you which piece is attacking which piece.

The correct answer for diagram 22.4 is that the white bishop is attacking a black pawn.

If your child needs more practice, set up similar positions, making sure only one piece is attacking another.

Now set up a position where two pieces are attacked.

Diagram 22.5

Here the black queen is attacking the white knight and the black bishop is attacking the white pawn.

As your child gets better and better, you can add in more attackers. Once they have it down, you can show them a position like this:

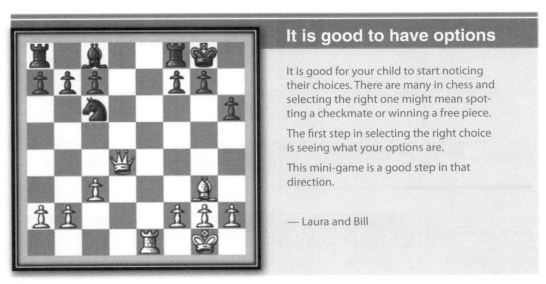

It is good to have options

It is good for your child to start noticing their choices. There are many in chess and selecting the right one might mean spotting a checkmate or winning a free piece.

The first step in selecting the right choice is seeing what your options are.

This mini-game is a good step in that direction.

— Laura and Bill

Diagram 22.6

In diagram 22.6, the black knight is attacking the white queen and the white bishop is attacking a black pawn. The white queen is also attacking two black pawns.

For the purpose of this mini-game, it doesn't matter if it is a good move to take a particular piece. For instance, in the position above, the white queen would not want to take either black pawn. This would be a bad trade. Still, it is good for your child to notice that these captures are possible.

The only thing you want your child to do in this exercise is to spot that a piece can be taken. A player should always know their options.

With practice comes the ability to see when your piece is attacked and when you can take another piece.

This can give you a huge advantage in chess, as it is easier to win when you have more pieces than your opponent.

Step 3: Let's play!

Discuss with your child that there are two ways they might be able to take a piece. Either they can attack a piece or the other player might just move their piece onto a square that they protect.

Play a game with your child. When you get to a certain point in the game, ask your child, "Okay, now what pieces are being attacked?" Have them point to all the pieces. There probably will be many!

Keep playing and, after six or seven more moves, ask them to show you all the pieces under attack.

Continue with this exercise throughout the game. When they can easily point to all the pieces that are attacked, not missing any, you can move on to the next chapter.

 **Troubleshooting Tips**

Problem:
My child has trouble finding all the pieces that are being attacked.

Solution:

Start with fewer pieces on the board. Find the point where they can easily spot what pieces are attacking other pieces. Then add a few more pieces and quiz them on these positions. Only add pieces when they are confident with the easier exercises.

Problem:

My child is selecting pieces that aren't attacked.

Solution:

Ask your child which piece is attacking the piece they selected. If they name a piece, make sure they understand how that piece moves. If they have trouble with that piece's movements, these mini-games will be extremely difficult.

If they shrug their shoulders, it is possible that they are just guessing. You'll need to uncover what the problem is. If you're on Step 3, go back to Step 2 and set up more examples. If they're having trouble with Step 2, go back to Step 1. Spend more time here, starting with positions with just a few pieces.

If they are having trouble with Step 1, have them point to all the squares where the attacking piece can move. If they are missing squares where this piece can go, review the chapter on that piece.

More About
DEFENDING

23

hen one of your pieces is attacked, there are four things you can do to protect it:

1. *Move away*
2. *Block*
3. *Support*
4. *Take*

It is important that your child is familiar with each of these four basic methods of dealing with an attack.

1. *Move away* – move the piece so that it is no longer being attacked.
2. *Block* – move another piece between the piece being attacked and the attacking piece.
3. *Support* – move a piece so that it could "take the taker."
4. *Take* – capture the attacking piece.

They should understand all four choices, so that they can use them in a game to protect their pieces.

Step 1: Let's review a little

In Chapter 8, "How to Attack and Defend Pieces," your child learned that they can move away or support a piece to get out of danger.

Review those concepts with your child. Show a few examples of each. Have your child show you a few examples.

Now tell them that there are two other ways they can protect a piece.

Step 2: A piece can block

Another way to protect is to use your pieces to block an attack.

Set up this position:

Diagram 23.1

In diagram 23.1, the white bishop is attacking the black queen. The black queen can move away, but Black can also block.

Show your child that the black bishop can block here:

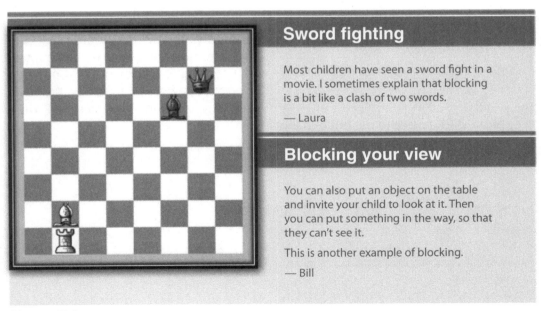

Diagram 23.2

Explain that "block" means to get in the way in order to stop the attack.

Show your child that in diagram 23.2 White can take the black bishop, but then Black can take back. It will be an even trade of a bishop for a bishop.

Here is another example you can show your child.

Diagram 23.3

Here the black bishop is attacking the white pawn. Help your child to see that White can block to protect the pawn.

Diagram 23.4

Explain to your child that if the black bishop were to take the pawn, the other pawn would take back. Black would be trading a bishop for a pawn, which isn't a good trade. That's why this move protects the white pawn.

Set up other positions where Black or White can block to protect a piece from attack.

Step 3: Mini-game: You block

Now give your child a chance to show you that they can block. Set up positions and have your child find the move that will block.

Here are more examples, with White to move in diagram 23.5, Black to move in diagram 23.6, and White to move in diagram 23.7:

First step

The first step in this mini-game is to spot the white piece that is attacked. This will be a good review of the last chapter.

— Laura

One rook supports the other

It is good to point out that the rooks support each other, which makes it possible for one to block the attack on the knight. Otherwise, the queen would just take the rook.

— Bill

Diagram 23.5

Only real option

When you set up this position, go over Black's options to save the queen. Can it move?

Also explore the idea of taking the rook. White would take back. Black would get a rook in exchange for a queen. Is that a good plan?

These are all little reviews of previous concepts.

— Laura and Bill

Diagram 23.6

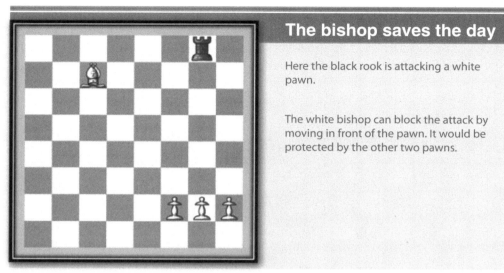

The bishop saves the day

Here the black rook is attacking a white pawn.

The white bishop can block the attack by moving in front of the pawn. It would be protected by the other two pawns.

Diagram 23.7

Step 4: Sometimes you can take the attacker!

Tell your child that there are times when you can just take the piece that is attacking you. Sometimes you can take it for free!

Set up this example:

Beginners move away

It is very common for beginners to move their piece away when it is attacked. It is a natural response.

This step will help your child see that they need to explore all their options. In this case, White can just take the rook without being taken back.

— Laura and Bill

Diagram 23.8

Explain that in this situation the black rook is attacking the white knight. It is White's turn. What should White do? Discuss options with your child.

One possible solution is to block with the bishop. Since you just went over blocking, that might be fresh in their mind. Talk about this with your child. What would Black do? It is good if they can spot that Black would just take the bishop. These sorts of calculations are what chess is all about.

You can start by asking your child to name all the pieces that are being attacked. It's a good review of the last chapter.

The option of simply taking the attacker is often overlooked by beginners. They see that their piece is attacked and they move it. It is good to be able to see when the attacker can be taken.

Show them other examples where they can take the attacker. Here's another:

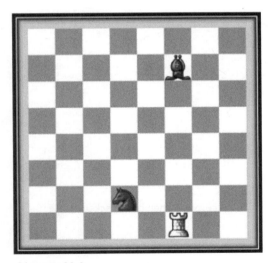

Diagram 23.9

Have your child play Black. Ask what piece of theirs is under attack. Now ask what they can do about it. The best answer is to take the white rook with the black knight. However, moving the bishop will get them out of danger.

Also make sure to include positions where a pawn can take the attacker.

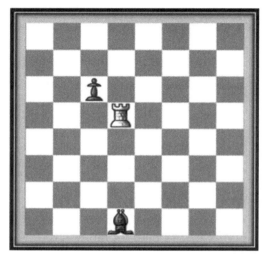

Diagram 23.10

Show them more examples of this.

Step 5: Mini-game: You take

Set up positions for your child, telling them which side to play. Ask them how they can take the attacker in each position.

Here are some examples:

Here your child is playing Black. Ask what piece of theirs is under attack. Now ask them if they can find a way to take the attacker.

Diagram 23.11

It is good to set up a few positions where a pawn can take the attacker. This is often missed by beginners.

Diagram 23.12

In diagram 23.12, you'd have your child play White. Ask them how they can take the attacker. You can also ask them which pieces are under attack, making sure they see that both the rook and the bishop are being attacked.

Diagram 23.13

In diagram 23.13, they will be playing White. Ask them what they should do about the attack on the knight.

Diagram 23.14

In diagram 23.14, you'll ask your child to play White. What piece can they take to get out of danger?

Set up more positions like this and ask your child to find the piece that can take the attacker. In the beginning you can give them hints by asking questions like, "Which piece is being attacked?" or, "Can you take the piece that is attacking you?"

When they start easily seeing that the best solution is to just take the attacker, go to the next section.

Step 6: Mini-game: Show the four ways

It is a good idea to quiz them on the four methods to protect a piece:

- Move away
- Block
- Support
- Take

Ask your child to show these four methods to you.

If they have trouble, show them examples of each of the ways they can handle an attack. Then ask them to show you examples.

Step 7: Mini-game: What would you do?

Now we're going to look at some more positions, ones that might come up in a game. In each position, a piece is attacked and one of the four methods of protecting is best.

Here is what you'll do for each position:

1) Tell them which side they are playing (White or Black) and set the board up so they are facing the correct position.

2) Have them tell you which of their pieces is under attack.

3) Ask them to show you which methods are available in this position.

4) Work with them to find the best solution in the given position.

We'll give the correct answer next to the diagram for you to reference.

Sample positions

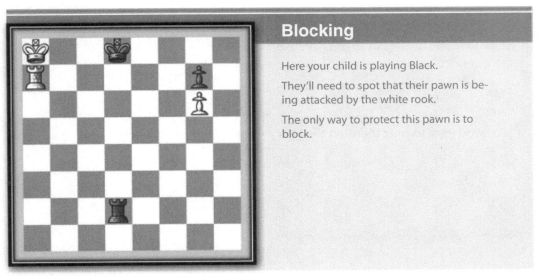

Blocking

Here your child is playing Black.

They'll need to spot that their pawn is being attacked by the white rook.

The only way to protect this pawn is to block.

Diagram 23.15

Diagram 23.16

Take the attacker

Here your child is playing White.

Their pawn is being attacked by the black bishop.

In this position, White can block, move away, or take the attacker.

Discuss these options with your child and help them work out the best solution.

Diagram 23.17

Support that pawn!

Here they are playing Black.

Once they spot that their pawn is attacked by the white bishop, they will need to recognize there is only one way to save it.

They must move the king to support the pawn.

This is a good example, as it combines the concept of the long diagonal with the idea that the king can support a piece.

Diagram 23.18

Moving to promote

Here they are playing Black. They only have a king and one piece and look to be terribly behind.

Fortunately their pawn is about to promote. When they move the pawn, they get out of danger *and* they get a queen!

Diagram 23.19

Protect by blocking

Here your child is playing White.

The only answer to the attack on their pawn is to block with another pawn.

It is good to give a few of these examples, as this theme comes up frequently in chess games.

Take with the king

Tell your child that they are playing Black.

The correct answer is that the black king can take the white rook.

It is good to give your child other examples, like this, where the king is active in the position. Beginners often forget that they can take pieces with their king.

Diagram 23.20

Create more examples like this to quiz your child. Some positions can have more than one solution, while others can simply have one choice.

This is a mini-game to play over and over with your child. These positions will help tremendously.

Step 8: Let's play!

Now it is a good idea to play a few games with these concepts in mind. Have fun with it. When a piece is attacked, talk about the solutions available to protect that piece.

Troubleshooting Tips

Problem:
My child doesn't get the concept of blocking.

Solution:

You can tell them that "blocking" is just putting something in the way. Show them lots of real-life examples. For instance, you can set something on the table in front of them and then block it with your hand. Get them to see that your hand is in the way, so they can't see part of the object.

Show them many examples in chess. Ask your child what they would call this. Consult them on this point. If they want to call it, "putting something in the way," that's fine. The only important thing here is that they really understand that this is a way they can protect their pieces.

Problem:

On the mini-game, "Show the four ways," my child cannot show me the four ways to protect a piece.

Solution:

Show your child many examples of each of the four ways to protect a piece.

If your child still can't show the four ways they could protect a piece on their own, they probably don't understand something about one or more of the methods. In order to pinpoint the problem, set up a position that has all four methods available to them. Below is an example:

Diagram 23.21

Tell them that they are playing White in this position.

Ask your child, "Which piece is attacked?" If they have any trouble with this, do a review of the previous chapter. It is important that they can spot the attack.

Next, ask them to show you how they can protect their rook. See how many methods they can demonstrate to you on the board. If they come up with all four, that's great. That's really all you want.

If your child can't show you one (or more) of the ways, ask them about that method. For instance, you might say, "How would you block in this position?" If they have trouble with this, show them many more examples of blocking.

When you've completed this step, make sure they can now show you all four ways to get out of an attack.

Problem:
My child is having trouble finding the best solution in the mini-game, "What would you do?"

Solution:
As long as they understand the four methods, the solution is to give them many examples and talk to them about it. Find out what they think about each solution.

It takes a while to develop the skill of choosing the best options in chess. The first step is to see the choices available. If they are doing this, just go over more positions with them and they'll start to find the best solutions.

Problem:
My child always chooses "move away" as the option in the mini-game: What would you do?

Solution:
Make sure they completely understand the other three choices.

Consult them with each position and see if they can show you how to take an attacker, block an attack, and support a piece. Discuss the options with them, consulting their opinions and understanding of the choice.

Getting Out of Check

24

**tep 1: Let's review check and moving out of check**

1a. Here's check again: It is important to make sure that your child understands what "check" means and can spot check on a chessboard.

If you feel that a quick review would help, simply show them a few positions that are check and then ask them to show you a few.

1b. Moving out of check: Now review the step in Chapter 11, "Check," which goes over how to move the king out of check.

Let your child know that moving the king away is one way to handle check. There are two others.

Step 2: You can take the attacker to get out of check

Beginners often forget that they might be able to take the attacker when they are in check. A child's first instinct is often to move the king. For this reason, it is a good idea to spend some time on this section and show many examples.

First start with positions where the king can simply take the piece which has it in check.

Set up the following position:

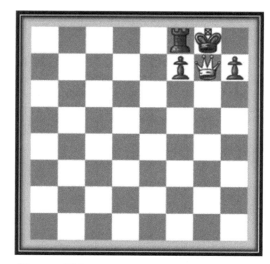

Diagram 24.1

Discuss this position with your child. Many beginners will assume that this is checkmate, because the king cannot move away.

Help your child to see that the king can just take the queen, because it isn't protected by any other piece.

Now set up this position:

Don't just move away

Children often just move away when their king is attacked. It is a natural response.

The queen is very powerful when next to the king. It can seem impossible that the king could just take it.

It's important to show many examples. Then, when it comes up in a game, your child will ask, "Is that queen actually protected? No? I can take it!"

— Laura and Bill

Diagram 24.2

Point out that the white queen is checking the black king, but that nothing is protecting the queen. The black king can just take it.

Set up more examples showing how the king can get out of check by taking the attacker.

Also show positions where another piece can take the attacker. Here are a couple of examples:

Here the rook can just take the queen.

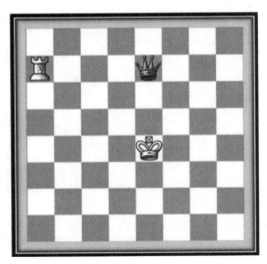

Diagram 24.3

In this position the knight can take the bishop.

Diagram 24.4

Step 3: Mini-game: Can you take the attacker?

Set up various positions where your child can take the attacker.

Here are a few examples:

Diagram 24.5

In this position, Black's rook is checking White's king. Ask, "Can White take the attacker?"

Diagram 24.6

Here Black's king is in check by White's powerful queen. Ask your child if the black king can take the queen.

Diagram 24.7

The black bishop is checking the white king. What can White do about it?

Diagram 24.8

The black knight has put the white king in check. Can White take the attacker?

Diagram 24.9

Here the white rook is attacking the black king. Can Black take the attacker?

Step 4: Here's how you can block to get out of check

Explain to your child that you can block an attack on the king to get the king out of check.

Set up this example:

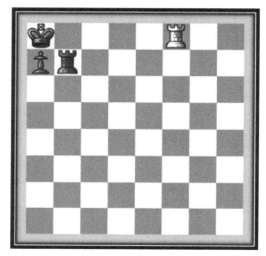

Diagram 24.10

Ask your child to show you how the black king is in check. Go over with your child that the king can't move out of check.

Show them that the only way to get the king out of check in diagram 24.10 is to block the attack with the rook, by putting it between the king and the attacker:

Diagram 24.11

Set up more positions like this. Here's an example:

Here the black queen is checking the white king. Can White block to get out of check?

Diagram 24.12

Step 5: Mini-game: You block to get out of check

Now set up more positions and have your child find the correct blocking move to get out of check.

Here are two examples:

Diagram 24.13

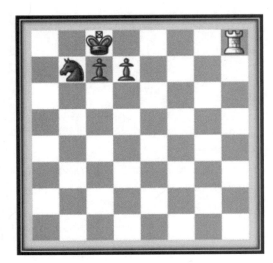

Diagram 24.14

Step 6: Mini-game: Show me the three ways a king can get out of check

Have your child set up positions that show you the three ways a king can get out of check.

Make sure they show you all three ways:

- Moving the king out of check
- Taking the attacker
- Blocking the check

Step 7: Mini-game: How should you get the king out of check?

Now quiz your child on different positions, showing different ways to get out of check.

Here are some sample positions:

Diagram 24.15

Here the white king must move to get out of check.

Diagram 24.16

Here Black must block to get out of check.

Diagram 24.17

Here White must take the queen to get out of check.

Once they have this down, show examples where the king has choices. Here are three positions:

Diagram 24.18

Here Black can either move the king or block with the bishop.

Diagram 24.19

Here the king can take the rook, or move away.

Here White can block with the rook or the king can move.

Diagram 24.20

You can also come up with positions where all options are available. Here's an example:

Here Black can block the check with the rook, take the rook with the bishop, or move away.

Diagram 24.21

Troubleshooting Tips

Problem:
My child tends to only move the king to get out of check when there are better options.

Solution:
Set up a lot of examples where they can block or take. Discuss with them the advantages of both. Sometimes moving the king out of check is the best solution. You just want them to know that there are options.

Problem:
My child has trouble finding how the king is in check.

Solution:
Review Chapter 11, "Check." It is important that they can see this easily for these mini-games.

Problem:
My child has trouble seeing attacks on the long diagonal.

Solution:
This is a common issue for beginners. If you spot this problem, give them many examples where a piece is attacking on a long diagonal. Show them positions where pieces are attacked by a bishop or queen, and positions where the king is in check along the diagonal.

Problem:
My child didn't see that a pawn could take an attacker.

Solution:
Show them many examples where a pawn takes the attacker to get out of check.

Problem:
My child continually moves the king into check.

Solution:
Review Chapter 11, "Check." Make sure that your child understands when the king is in check and when it isn't. Spend some time on the various mini-games in that chapter.

More About
CHECKMATE

25

We touched on checkmate earlier, but there's a lot more for your child to learn about this concept.

Checkmate is tricky. It takes time and practice to master.

Since you can only win by checkmating the other player, it's important to fully understand this concept.

Now that your child has a good understanding of the subjects covered in the previous chapters, they will be able to grasp the concept of checkmate much easier.

Once you know they have these elements down, you can really explore checkmate!

Review checkmate

Do a rapid review of Chapter 12, "Checkmate." It's important for your child to understand all these concepts well before starting on this chapter.

Step 1: This is how you figure out if a position is checkmate

Your child must learn to be able to tell when a position is checkmate. You can give your child a tool to help them figure out, for themselves, if they really have checkmate.

1a: Why is this so important? Explain the importance of knowing when a king is checkmated. If it's your king, you need to know if there's a threat. You need to know if the other player is about to win the game.

If you are analyzing the other player's position, you need to know that your plan will end in victory. Is the final position you're envisioning actually checkmate?

Let your child know that spotting checkmates takes practice. It's not going to be an overnight process.

1b: The Checkmate Checklist: Go over this Checkmate Checklist with your child:

1) Is the king in check?

If the answer is no, stop here. Remember, it isn't checkmate if it isn't check!

2) Can the attacker be taken?

If the attacking piece can be taken, it isn't checkmate.

3) Can the king move out of check?

For this step, you need to run through a mental list of all the squares surrounding the king. If the king can move to a square that isn't being attacked, it isn't checkmate.

4) Is it possible to block?

If you can block the check, it isn't checkmate. Beginning players often overlook this.

The only purpose of this checklist is to determine if a position is or is not checkmate.

Have your child repeat the checklist back to you. It should be easy, as they know the basic ways to get out of check from the previous chapter, "Getting out of Check."

Step 2: Let's try out the checklist

Now work with your child to figure out if the following positions are checkmate, using the checklist. Start with positions where the king is in the corner of the board, like so:

Some of these positions will be checkmate, some will not.

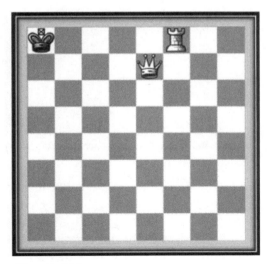

Diagram 25.1

Your child will be familiar with this checkmate position, so this will be easier for them.

Still, go through the checklist with them, as it will give them practice using it.

Diagram 25.2

In Chapter 12, "Checkmate," we stuck with rooks and queens. Now you should add in other pieces.

Here the king is in check, and the attacker cannot be taken, but it can move out of check.

Diagram 25.3

This is similar to a position from the early chapter, "Checkmate." Adding a bishop makes it a little more complicated, but it is still checkmate.

Diagram 25.4

This is a good one to add, because it comes up a lot. Children think it is checkmate, because the king can't move.
When they do the checklist, they see that the king isn't in check. All you want to do here is get them to see that this isn't checkmate.

Now add a few more pieces into the position, keeping the king in the corner.

Here are two examples:

Diagram 25.5

Diagram 25.6

The solution of blocking the checkmate with the bishop might be overlooked if your child didn't use the checklist. The white bishop is far away, which makes it harder to see.

Here, the checkmate is similar to what they have seen, but the way the king's escape squares are covered is a bit different. Adding in the other pieces makes it a new challenge. Your child will need to figure out if these interfere with the checkmate.

Show your child more examples like this, where the king is still in the corner, but you're adding in new pieces to make it more complex.

When your child is comfortable using this checkmate checklist, go to the next step.

Step 3: Here's another kind of checkmate

Now we're going to show a different checkmate theme. Set up this position:

Diagram 25.7

Here the king is not in the corner. You'll want to point out to your child that there are more escape squares, so it is harder to checkmate the king.

Run through the checkmate checklist with your child, to help them see that this is checkmate. Tell your child that this is a common checkmate that they will see in games.

Discuss with your child why this checkmate works. Point out that the queen is protected, so the king can't take it. Then look at all the other squares around the king. Show your child that the queen covers each square.

Now take the rook off the board, like so:

Diagram 25.8

Discuss with your child how this position is very different now. Why? What did taking the rook off the board do?

Show your child other checkmates similar to this. Here are some examples:

Diagram 25.9

Diagram 25.10

You don't need to check all of the squares each time, but it is good to go through the checklist a few times. This is a familiar pattern. Show your child many examples like these.

Step 4: Mini-game: Why isn't this checkmate?

Now show your child positions similar to the ones in the previous step, but which aren't actually checkmate. Using the checklist, have them tell you why it isn't.

Here are some examples:

Diagram 25.11

Here Black can move out of check.

Diagram 25.12

Here White is not in check, so it isn't checkmate.

Diagram 25.13

Here Black can move out of check.

This one is good to reinforce with many examples. Beginners often make the mistake of putting their queen next to a king, thinking that they have checkmated.

It is very disappointing to lose one's queen in a winning position.

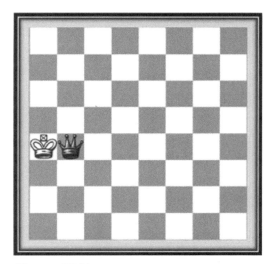

Diagram 25.14

Step 5: Mini-game: Is this checkmate?

Now quiz your child on whether a position is or isn't checkmate, based on these new kinds of checkmates. Here are some examples, similar to the positions just discussed:

Diagram 25.15

This is checkmate.

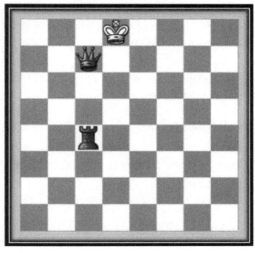

Diagram 25.16

This is not checkmate.

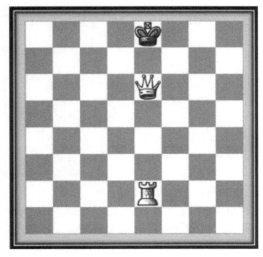

Diagram 25.17

This is not checkmate.

Come up with more examples, until your child can quickly spot them correctly.

Step 6: Mini-game: You set up checkmate

Now have your child set up similar positions of checkmate. They can be any style, using any number of pieces. It's fine if they stick with the two themes you just went over. These are common and useful.

If your child sets up a position that isn't checkmate, have them go through their checklist.

Then have them correct the position, so that it is checkmate.

Step 7: Here's how it might look in a game

Show your child a few examples of this type of checkmate in a position they might see in a game.

Diagram 25.18

This checkmate theme is very common in a game.

Diagram 25.19

It is important to show examples for both sides (White and Black).

Step 8: Let's play!

Now that you've gone over these fundamental checkmates, it is a good idea to play a few games. It is possible that the checkmate themes that we have discussed will come up, especially if your child is looking out for them.

Step 9: Here's another checkmate you'll see a lot

Let your child know that there are other checkmates that are very common.

Set up this position:

Diagram 25.20

Discuss this kind of checkmate with your child. Go through the checklist.

Point out that this is checkmate. Have your child look at all the squares around the king.

Show your child that Black's pawns block three squares in front of the king.

Now show them more checkmates along this line. Here is another example that is slightly different:

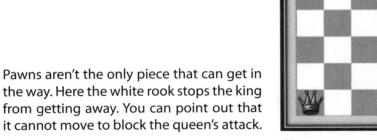

Diagram 25.21

Pawns aren't the only piece that can get in the way. Here the white rook stops the king from getting away. You can point out that it cannot move to block the queen's attack.

Step 10: Mini-game: Why isn't this checkmate?

Now show your child similar positions which are not checkmate. Here's an example:

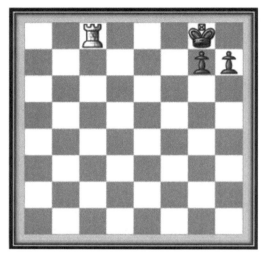

Diagram 25.22

If you go through the Checkmate Checklist, your child will see that the king can move out of check.

Diagram 25.23

Show your child how the king can move out of danger, because one of the pawns has been pushed. This is a common way to avoid checkmate.

Diagram 25.24

Here Black can block the check with the rook.

Show your child more positions similar to these. Make sure to alternate between putting the black and white kings in check.

Step 11: Is this checkmate?

Set up positions, similar to the ones we went over in Step 9 and 10, asking, "Is this checkmate?"

Here are some examples:

Diagram 25.25

This is not checkmate.

Diagram 25.26

This is checkmate.

Step 12: You set up checkmate

Now have your child set up positions like this on their own. Run through the Checkmate Checklist with them, helping them to make sure their checkmates work.

Step 13: This is how it might look in a game

Now show your child a few examples of this type of checkmate, which might appear in a game. Here are two examples:

Diagram 25.27

Here the white rook is checkmating the black king.

Diagram 25.28

Here the black rook is checkmating the white king.

Show your child more examples like this.

Step 14: Mini-game: Can you find checkmate in one move?

Now using the different kinds of checkmates that we went over, set up positions where they need to find the correct move to checkmate the other player.

Start with ones that are very simple, sticking with the last theme discussed.

Tell your child which side can be checkmated.

Then give them time to look over the position. Don't let them puzzle over any one position for too long. Instead, show them the correct answer and set up another one similar to it.

Here are some examples of simple checkmate-in-one positions:

Diagram 25.29

Tell your child that Black can be checkmated in one move. Since there are fewer pieces on the board, it will be easier for them to spot the right answer.

Then you can begin to add more and more pieces to the position.

Diagram 25.30

Here White can be checkmated in one move.

It will be easier for your child to spot the correct answer if you create a position where the queen moves straight down the board, rather than on the diagonal.

Diagram 25.31

Let your child know that White can be checkmated in one move. Here you have simply moved the queen to a different square. They will need to find the checkmate by moving the queen along the diagonal. Since they solved a similar position in the last diagram, it will be easier for them to spot this now.

Show them a few more examples like this, which are simple checkmate-in-one positions.

Next, quiz them on the other theme you went over. Set up simple positions like these:

Diagram 25.32

Let them know that White can checkmate Black in one move.

Your child might need help remembering this checkmate pattern. The white queen can take the pawn to checkmate Black.

Here Black can checkmate White in one move. Since this is the same theme as the previous puzzle, they are likely to get it.

Diagram 25.33

Start adding in more and more pieces until you have one that looks like this:

Let your child know that Black can checkmate White in one move.

If they need help, point out the black bishop to your child. Since it is far away from the white king, it can get forgotten.

Diagram 25.34

Come up with as many positions like this as you can. They are invaluable for your child's chess education!

Step 15: Let's Play!

Now play a few more games. If you see these positions come up, point them out to your child.

Troubleshooting Tips

Problem:
My child cannot figure out why a position isn't checkmate.

Solution:
Help your child run through the Checkmate Checklist. Discuss each point as necessary. If they have trouble with a particular point, go back over the appropriate section in this book. For instance, if they have trouble spotting how a piece can block to get out of checkmate, review sections covering this in Chapter 24, "Getting out of Check."

Problem:
My child cannot figure out if a position is checkmate.

Solution:
Help your child run through the Checkmate Checklist. Go through it point by point, working with them to see if the position is checkmate.

Start with very simple positions.

If your child has trouble with this, make sure they understand what checkmate is. If they have trouble with that, go back to Chapter 12, "Checkmate," earlier in this book.

Remember that it takes a while to get this down. You may need to run through dozens of positions in each mini-game of this chapter. Even though the positions are similar, these exercises will help your child to become skilled in correctly identifying checkmate.

Problem:
When we play, "Is this checkmate?" my child always answers "yes."

Solution:
This is often a sign that they don't really understand what is going on.

Ask them what checkmate means and have them set up a checkmate for you. If they can't do this, review Chapter 12, "Checkmate," with your child.

If they can set up a checkmate, have them run through the Checkmate Checklist with you for the particular checkmate that they set up. Then run through the Checkmate Checklist on a few other positions which are not checkmate.

If you discuss each point of the checklist with them in detail, you should uncover any problems or confusion they may have on the earlier steps, allowing you to do appropriate exercises to help them with those points.

Problem:
My child is having trouble figuring out checkmate-in-one positions.

Solution:
Start with positions which have fewer pieces on the board. Positions with more pieces are harder. For instance, this position is more difficult:

Diagram 25.35

A similar position, with many pieces taken off, is easier:

Diagram 25.36

The concept of the checkmate is the same, but one is much easier to figure out than the other.

Keep creating positions that are very similar to this, until they can spot the answers easily. Repetition is key here. You cannot overdo these exercises.

Problem:
My child is having trouble with Step 3 of the checklist (figuring out if the king can move out of checkmate).

Solution:
This is a tricky part of figuring out if you have checkmate. This skill takes practice, and usually develops over time. However, if you see that they are struggling, there are some exercises that you can do to isolate the skills involved.

The first step is to make sure your child can figure out the squares where the king can move, disregarding the element of check. Review "Step 3: Point to the squares where the king can go" in Chapter 21, "Your Own Pieces Can Get in the Way."

Set up examples that will help them with the mini-games in the present chapter.

Here are some examples. For each position, have your child point out the squares where the king can go:

Diagram 25.37

Diagram 25.38

It is good for your child to recognize that there is an extra escape square offered by the pushed pawn.

The second step is to make sure that they can quickly tell if the king is in check. Review "Step 3: Is this check?" from Chapter 11, "Check," to be sure they can quickly identify when the king is in check.

The third step is to review "Step 6: Can the king go here?" in Chapter 11, "Check." Add in positions that relate to this current chapter. For instance, you can set up this position:

Ask your child about all the squares around the king. You can also include the squares occupied by the black pawns, just to drive home the point that these squares were taken away by Black's own pieces. Make sure your child spots the escape square created by the pushed pawn.

Diagram 25.39

Stalemate and Draw

26

tep 1: Sometimes neither player wins the game

Explain to your child that in chess there are times when neither side can win. It isn't important to go over many examples of this. Basically, if you can't checkmate the other player, you can't win.

In other games, this might be called a tie, but in chess we call this a "draw."

Here is an example that is clearly a draw:

Diagram 26.1

Show your child that, since a king cannot attack another king (without putting itself in danger), there is no way for either side to checkmate the other.

Go over how this would be a draw. No one wins, no one loses.

A draw can also be agreed upon by two players. One player offers a draw and the other accepts it.

Step 2: This is stalemate

Explain to your child that when one side cannot make a legal move and that side's king is not in check, it's a draw. This special kind of draw is called "stalemate."

This can be a confusing concept, so make sure to provide lots of examples of stalemate (as well as examples of positions that are not).

Here is a good place to start:

Diagram 26.2

Beginners will often hit this position in a game. If it's White's turn, White cannot make a legal move. Explain to your child that this is stalemate because there are no legal moves yet White is not in check.

However, if it is Black's move, it isn't stalemate. Black can move.

Once they see that, show them this position:

Diagram 26.3

Explain that this is not stalemate because White does have a legal move (White can move the pawn). It is important that your child understands that stalemate isn't just that the king cannot move, but that one side cannot make any legal move.

Here are more examples of stalemate:

Diagram 26.4

Diagram 26.5

Here it is Black's turn. Go over all the possible squares where the king could go, and make sure your child sees why the king can't go to any of them.

This is not checkmate because the white king is not in check. This is stalemate because the white king is not in check yet White has no legal moves.

Diagram 26.5 is similar to the other positions you went over with your child in the chapter called, "Checkmate." It's good to point out stalemates where the king is in the corner, because there are fewer squares where it can go.

Discuss the positions with your child. Ask them who was ahead. Who has more pieces and who would have won had it not been stalemate? In these positions, the side that stalemated the other player should have won.

Stalemate can happen a lot when someone tries to get too many queens. Beginners love to load up the board with queens. It can be hard not to stalemate the other player when you have so much firepower, when the other side has little or none!

Step 3: Mini-game: Is this stalemate?

Now show your child positions and ask, "Is this stalemate?" Make sure to include a lot of examples that aren't stalemate, such as positions where:

- The king is in check and can move.
- One side is in checkmate.
- One side cannot move their king, but they can make another legal move.

The positions shouldn't involve many pieces and should just show the basic themes. The important thing is that your child learns to spot when there is a stalemate.

When your child can spot this very quickly, without errors, you know they have this concept down.

Even so, this is a mini-game to revisit again and again.

Step 4: Mini-game: Is this check, checkmate, or stalemate?

Show your child various positions, similar to the ones in the mini-game from Step 3, and have them tell you which are check, checkmate, and stalemate.

Here are some examples:

Diagram 26.6

This is checkmate.

Diagram 26.7

This is stalemate.

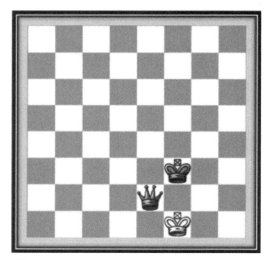

Diagram 26.8

This is check.

When your child does the Checkmate Checklist, they will notice that the king can move out of check. As a side note, you could point out that when the white king moves to the one square where it can go, Black can checkmate on the next move. See if they can spot that mate.

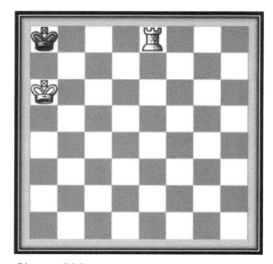

Diagram 26.9

This is checkmate.

Diagram 26.10

This is stalemate.

Diagram 26.11

Diagram 26.12

This is check. White can move out of check, so it is not checkmate.

This is checkmate.

You'll want to come up with many examples like this. It is okay if the themes are repeated over and over. The common ones will come up in many of their games.

If your child wants to come up with examples of their own and quiz you, encourage this. It would help them tremendously to compose these positions and figure out with you if they are check, checkmate, or stalemate.

In the end, your child needs to learn how to identify check, checkmate, and stalemate quickly, so work on increasing the speed of this mini-game.

This is another mini-game that you can review over and over with benefit.

Troubleshooting Tips

Problem:
My child doesn't understand what stalemate is.

Solution:

Review the first step of the Checkmate Checklist. Discuss it with them. Make sure they understand that check is an important part of checkmate.

Next, show them an example where one side cannot move. Have them pretend that they are playing Black here and that it is their turn:

Diagram 26.13

Now ask your child, "Are you in check?" Make sure they see that it isn't check. If they feel it is, do a rapid review of Chapter 11, "Check." Once they see that this isn't check, continue.

Now point to each square around the black king and ask, "Can the black king move here?" Make sure they understand that the king has no legal move. If they have trouble spotting whether the king is in check, review "Step 3: Is this check?" from Chapter 11, "Check," to be sure they can quickly identify when the king is in check.

You might also review "Step 6: Can the king go here?" in Chapter 11, "Check."

Once they understand that the king isn't in check and that it can't move, simply tell them that this is stalemate and is a draw.

Set up this position in another corner and ask, "Is this stalemate?" Have them explain to you why it is stalemate.

Problem:
My child confuses checkmate with stalemate.

Solution:
This is a common confusion with beginning chess players.

The key difference is that when a king is in checkmate, it must be in check. And if the king is in check, it cannot be stalemate.

Show your child many examples of both checkmate and stalemate. It helps to create positions that are very similar, and show why one position is checkmate and why one is stalemate.

For instance, this is stalemate:

Diagram 26.14

Make sure that your child sees that the king is not in check here, but cannot move (and Black doesn't have any other pieces to move).

Now show them this position:

Diagram 26.15

Tell them that this one is checkmate and the other is stalemate. Ask them to tell you the difference between the two positions. Why is the second one checkmate?

Show them more positions like this. When you feel that they have this down, have your child show you examples of checkmate and stalemate, explaining to you the difference between the two.

Problem:
My child has trouble telling check and checkmate apart.

Solution:
Review Chapter 25, "More About Checkmate," focusing on the mini-games there. Give your child many examples of positions that are just check and positions that are checkmate. Go over why one is checkmate and the other is not.

This takes a lot of practice, and these mini-games should be revisited again and again. As your child gains experience, they will see new nuances in these positions and mini-games, and will learn more from them.